D0536712

SIZZLING STIR-FRIES

KAY FAIRFAX

PHOTOGRAPHS BY
ROBIN MATTHEWS

RIZZOLI
NEW YORK

CONTENTS

THE PANTRY

Many of the ingredients used in this book are not standard kitchen cupboard items, and several may be new to you. But once you have mastered the simple art of stir-frying you will want to experiment and become more adventurous with varied flavors and textures. Most stir-fry recipes use the best fresh ingredients with large amounts of seasonal vegetables and fruit, smaller portions of lean meat, poultry, fish, and seafood. If you have a selection of sauces, spices, nuts, rice, and noodles in the cupboard already, you can create a new inspired taste sensation in less than one hour from arriving home to sitting down to a fabulous meal. Remember that the list here is only a guide, and should be tailored to suit your own requirements.

SPICES
Whole Black Peppercorns, Whole Red Peppercorns, Sea Salt, Chinese Five-Spice Powder

DRY INGREDIENTS
Cornstarch, Bouillon cubes (Chicken, Beef, Fish, and Vegetable), Brown Sugar, Dried Chinese Mushrooms, Dried Citrus Peel

CANNED GOODS
Water Chestnuts, Bamboo Shoots, Pineapple in Natural Juice

OIL AND VINEGAR
White-Wine Vinegar, Peanut Oil (also known as Groundnut Oil), Sesame Oil, Walnut Oil, Hazelnut Oil, Macadamia Nut Oil, Pistachio Oil

NUTS AND SEEDS
Sesame Seeds, Pine Nuts, Unsalted Peanuts, Unsalted Cashew Nuts, Almonds (whole and slivered), Walnuts, Hazelnuts, Pecans, Macadamia Nuts

NOODLES
Bean Thread Noodles (clear and transparent), Rice Noodles (opaque or clear white), Soft Fresh Noodles, Chinese Egg Noodles (round, not flat), Rice Vermicelli

RICE
Long-Grain White Rice, Brown Rice, Red Camargue Rice

SOY SAUCE
Made from fermented soybeans, flour, and water. (It has a pronounced salty flavor so you will probably not need to add salt to recipes with soy sauce.)

OTHER FLAVORINGS
Pale Dry Sherry, Shaoxing Wine

OYSTER SAUCE
A thick, rich brown sauce made from oysters cooked in brine and soy sauce. It does not have a strong fishy taste. Available at Asian grocery stores. Once opened it is best kept in the refrigerator.

FISH SAUCE
A thin, clear, salty sauce with a strong smell and flavor. Available at Asian grocery stores. Once opened it is best kept in the refrigerator.

HOISIN SAUCE
A thick, dark, sweet and spicy sauce made from soybeans. Available at supermarkets and Asian food stores. Once opened it is best kept in the refrigerator.

CHILI SAUCE
Made from hot chilis, this is bright red and HOT so use sparingly or dilute with a little hot water if it is too strong. Use according to personal taste.

CHILI BEAN SAUCE
A dark, thick, spicy sauce which can vary from mild to very hot, so use sparingly until you find the degree of "heat" you enjoy.

SWEET CHILI SAUCE
A sweet sauce usually with the chili seeds left in.

BLACK BEAN SAUCE
A smooth sauce made from fermented soybeans.

YELLOW BEAN SAUCE
This sauce is available in two varieties: whole beans or crushed beans. It is a thick, salty, spicy sauce.

SWEET-AND-SOUR SAUCE
Combines well with meat, chicken, fish, and vegetables. A deep, orange-red, this is made from red peppers, tomatoes, vinegar, garlic, and ginger. Not too hot or spicy.

TAMARIND SAUCE
A thick, brown and tangy sauce with a slightly acid flavor, but not bitter. Available at Asian grocery stores.

TERIYAKI SAUCE
Similar to Japanese soy sauce.

PESTO SAUCE
This Italian sauce is a wonderful green color and is made from fresh basil, pine nuts, garlic, olive oil, salt, and freshly ground black pepper.

TOMATO SAUCE
No explanation needed but make sure you buy a good-quality sauce.

WORCESTERSHIRE SAUCE
Flavored with anchovies, this thin sauce adds a distinctive "savory" flavor to dishes that include it.

WOKS AND STIR-FRY PANS

It is best to buy a wok that is at least 12 or 14 inches in diameter because it is much easier to toss food around in a large pan than a small one. The rounded-bottom woks can only be used on gas, but there are now many flat-bottomed designs to use on all fuel surfaces, so check carefully before buying. The exact cooking time will vary depending on which pan or wok you use, so you may have to slightly adjust the cooking times given in the recipes to suit your wok or pan.

CARBON STEEL WOK
This is not an expensive item to buy and is superior to the stainless-steel or aluminum woks. It can take high heat without burning itself or the food. Remember it must be seasoned before using the first time.

STAINLESS STEEL/ALUMINUM/CAST IRON
I do not recommend stainless steel or aluminum woks because I find they burn and smoke at high temperatures, and I find the cast iron too heavy to handle easily.

NONSTICK
These are suitable for stir-frying, but they cannot take as high a temperature as carbon steel, and you must remember not to use metal utensils or scourers because they will damage the nonstick coating.

FLAT-BOTTOMED, HIGH-SIDED PAN
Any flat-bottomed, high-sided pan can be used to stir-fry, but make sure the handle is long and does not become too hot to hold during cooking. The high sides make it easier to toss the ingredients.

SEASONING THE WOK

Before using a wok for the first time, it must be properly seasoned. First scrub the inside with a non-abrasive cleaner to remove any protective machine oil left on by the manufacturer, and dry well. Place the wok on the stove and, when warm and completely dry, coat the inside surface with vegetable oil (not olive oil). When the oil begins to smoke, remove the wok from the heat and allow it to cool. Using paper towels, wipe off all the excess oil. The paper will blacken. Repeat this oiling process 2 or 3 times, or until the paper wipes clean.

This process ensures the wok is properly seasoned and will not rust or burn. Always make sure the wok is completely dry after use and it is advisable to wipe the surface with a small amount of vegetable oil before storing. Never scrub the wok again, it should only be washed in hot water and wiped dry.

UTENSILS

Many of the following utensils may already be in your kitchen, but for successful stir-frying it is well worth investing in a few special pieces of equipment: a good-quality wok, very sharp knives, and a slotted spoon.

PEPPER GRINDER
This is used in most recipes, so choose a good-quality one that will coarsely grind the peppercorns and not just crush them into powder.

CHOPPING BOARDS
Wooden ones will prevent the countertop from being damaged and scratched. Use the plastic or white acrylic ones when chopping coriander, garlic, or any foods with a strong smell because they don't absorb the odor like a wooden one will.

SHARP KNIVES
Stir-frying entails a great deal of chopping and slicing, so have a good selection of knives and keep them sharp.

MINI CLEAVER
Buy a good quality stainless-steel mini cleaver. Once you become familiar with this traditional Chinese utensil you can use it to chop meat, crush garlic, and slice vegetables.

MINI WIRE WHISK
This is a great help for combining liquid and cornstarch before adding to the wok, and helps to make sure lumps do not occur in the sauce.

LONG-HANDLED METAL SLOTTED SPOON
Very useful in the removal of meat from the pan when cooking in batches.

BRASS WIRE SKIMMER
This is a traditional utensil used in wok cooking, but a long-handled slotted spoon is just as effective.

STAINLESS-STEEL STRAINER
Used for draining rice or noodles. I prefer the simple long-handled type.

STIFF SPLIT-BAMBOO BRUSH
A traditional brush used to clean the wok, but an ordinary soft plastic dishwashing brush is just as good.

PLASTIC SPATULA
This is a great for scraping out the last remains from the bowl or measuring cup.

LONG-HANDLED STAINLESS-STEEL WOK SPATULA
This is a long-handled curved metal spatula made for tossing meat and vegetables. It is shaped to the curve of the sides of the wok. It is easy to use, but only on carbon-steel surfaces, not on nonstick surfaces.

MEASURING PITCHERS
Invest in two or three different sized glass pitchers. A small one is very useful to combine lesser amounts, and is the most effective means of adding liquid to the pan, thus leaving one hand free to continue stirring.

MEASURING SPOONS
Most amounts used in stir-frying are small, so a variety of different sized spoons is very useful.

MIXING BOWLS
I prefer heavy glass bowls. These are especially useful for marinating, as well as for mixing the liquids.

GARLIC PRESS
Buy a good-quality one that is easy to clean, as this utensil is used in many stir-fry recipes.

MANDOLIN
This is very useful for making uniformly thin vegetable sticks. Ideal for carrots and zucchini.

KITCHEN SCISSORS
Many cooks find it easiest to snip parsley, chives, and other fresh herbs with sharp scissors rather than with a knife.

MEZZALUNA
This is my favorite utensil for chopping herbs, and I find it much quicker than other methods.

LONG-HANDLED WOODEN SPATULA
This resembles a flat salad server, and is a must for tossing the food in a wok or pan. Most importantly they are not abrasive on nonstick woks.

VEGETABLE PEELER
There are many types of vegetable peelers, so choose the one you are most comfortable with. An important utensil for preparing the vegetables and for zesting the citrus.

THE RECIPES

MEAT & POULTRY

Always buy tender, lean cuts of meat and poultry for stir-fry dishes because they are cooked so quickly. Although lean cuts are more expensive than tougher cuts, these recipes use much smaller proportions of meat to vegetables so it is not an extravagance. The finished dish will be tender and delicious. Meat and poultry are interchangeable for most of the recipes in this chapter.

BEEF, LETTUCE, AND NOODLES

This combination noodle soup is a great family dish. You can use any type of noodle in this recipe except vermicelli, which are too thin. Serves 4.

FOR THE MARINADE

1 teaspoon salt	*1 tablespoon sesame seeds*
Pinch of brown sugar	*1 tablespoon peanut oil*
3 tablespoons light soy sauce	*1 chili, seeded and finely sliced*
2 teaspoons pale dry sherry	*2 garlic cloves, sliced*
2 tablespoons sesame oil	*1 cup water*
2 tablespoons water	*1 head Iceberg or Romaine lettuce, separated*
1 teaspoon cornstarch	*into leaves, or Chinese cabbage*
5 turns of freshly ground black pepper	*2 scallions, finely sliced*

1 pound beef tenderloin, cut ¼ inch thick
9 ounces Chinese egg noodles

In a large bowl, combine the ingredients for the marinade. Add the beef and let marinate for 15 to 20 minutes.

Boil the noodles as directed on the package. Drain well and toss with the sesame seeds; set aside. Turn on the oven to its lowest setting.

Heat the wok. Add the peanut oil and, when the oil is very hot and begins to smoke, stir in the beef, the marinade, the chili, and garlic. Stir-fry 3 to 4 minutes. Using a slotted spoon, remove the beef; set aside in the oven. Add the water to the marinade in the wok and bring to a simmer. Add the lettuce and stir-fry 1 minute. Remove and arrange the leaves on top of noodles.

Return the beef to the wok with the scallions. Stir-fry 1 minute to reheat. Remove and place on top of the noodles and lettuce. Pour the remaining broth from the wok over the noodles, if desired.

PORK AND LYCHEE CURRY

This is a delicious combination of flavors and textures; the lychees add extra interest. Serve with white rice. Serves 4.

1 pound boneless pork, cut in	*3 tablespoons lychee syrup from the can*
bite-size chunks	*1 chili, seeded and finely chopped*
½ cup all-purpose flour	*2 bay leaves*
3 tablespoons peanut oil	*1 tablespoon fish sauce*
1 to 2 tablespoons green curry paste	*1 (15-ounce) can lychees*
1¾ cups coconut milk	

Toss the pork pieces in the flour and shake off any excess.

Heat the wok. Add the peanut oil and, when the oil is very hot and begins to smoke, add the pork pieces. Stir-fry 3 to 4 minutes, or until golden brown. Remove and drain on paper towels. Wipe out the wok to remove any remaining oil.

Reheat the wok. Add the curry paste and stir for 30 seconds, until mashed. Stir in the coconut milk and lychee syrup. Bring the liquid to a simmer. Add the chili, bay leaves, and fish sauce, stir-frying 2 minutes longer. Return the pork to the wok and add the lychees, letting everything simmer for a few minutes longer. Remove the bay leaves before serving.

CHICKEN LIVERS AND BACON

This is a marvelous appetizer or a light luncheon dish. Serve it on a bed of steamed white rice and sprinkle with chive flowers. Serves 4.

1 pound chicken livers, trimmed and	*1 tablespoon peanut oil*
chopped	*1 onion, finely chopped*
1 tablespoon pale dry sherry	*3 slices lean bacon, finely chopped*
2 teaspoons cornstarch	*1 tablespoon snipped fresh chives*
2 teaspoons water	*Freshly ground black pepper*

Soak the livers in a bowl of boiling water. Drain and repeat the process 2 or 3 times to eliminate any bitterness. Drain again and pat dry with paper towels.

In a small measuring pitcher, combine the sherry, cornstarch, and water. Heat the wok. Add the peanut oil and, when the oil is very hot and begins to smoke, add the onion and bacon. Stir-fry 1 minute. Add the livers and stir-fry 1 minute longer.

Remove the wok from the heat and stir in the cornstarch mixture. Return the wok to the heat and stir 1 minute. Add the chives and stir 30 seconds. Season with black pepper to taste.

Right: Beef, Lettuce, and Noodles

Duck and Orange

Duck and orange make a classic—and popular—combination. This super-quick dish has the extra crunch of snow peas. Serves 4.

1½ cups white long-grain rice	2 teaspoons pale dry sherry
2 teaspoons grated orange zest	2 oranges
1 pound duck breast half, cut into	1 tablespoon honey
½-inch-wide slices	3 tablespoons boiling water
½ teaspoon salt	1 tablespoon peanut oil
5 turns of freshly ground black pepper	3 ounces snow peas, trimmed
1 teaspoon cornstarch	

Cook the rice with 1 teaspoon of the orange zest in the cooking water. Drain well and keep hot. Marinate the duck slices in the salt, pepper, cornstarch, remaining orange zest, and 1 teaspoon of the sherry 15 minutes.

Meanwhile, peel the oranges and remove the skin from around the segments. Place these in a separate bowl with the remaining sherry; stir well. In another small bowl, mix together the honey and boiling water, stirring to dissolve the honey. Remove the duck pieces from the marinade and brush them with the honey and water mixture.

Heat the wok. Add the peanut oil and, when the oil is very hot and begins to smoke, add the duck and the marinade. Stir-fry 3 minutes. Add the oranges and snow peas and stir-fry 2 to 3 minutes longer. Remove from the heat and serve on a bed of hot rice.

Veal, Mushrooms, and Garlic

The ginger and cilantro give a hint of the Far East to this dish, as well as complement the flavor of the veal. Serves 4.

1 tablespoon pale dry sherry	1 pound veal, thinly sliced
1 teaspoon soy sauce	1½ cups zucchini, sliced diagonally
½ teaspoon cornstarch	2 cups sliced button mushrooms
2 tablespoons peanut oil	1 tablespoon chopped fresh cilantro
1 garlic clove, finely chopped	Freshly ground black pepper
1 teaspoon grated fresh gingerroot	

In a small measuring pitcher, combine the sherry, soy sauce, and cornstarch.

Heat the wok. Add the peanut oil and, when the oil is very hot and begins to smoke, add the garlic and ginger. Stir-fry 30 seconds. Add the veal and stir-fry 3 to 4 minutes longer, until brown and tender. Using a slotted spoon, remove the veal from the wok; set aside.

Return the wok to the heat. Add the zucchini and stir-fry 2 minutes. Add the mushrooms and stir-fry 1 minute longer. Stir in the cornstarch mixture and continue stir-frying 1 minute.

Return the veal to the wok. Stir-fry 1 minute, or until the vegetables are cooked but still crisp. Stir in the cilantro and season with pepper.

Lamb Navarin

Great at any time of year, this makes a particularly good spring lunch when served with a green salad. Serves 4.

1 tablespoon pale dry sherry	1½ cups long-grain white rice, boiled,
Finely shredded zest of 1 lemon	drained, and cooled
1 teaspoon sugar	3 scallions, finely sliced diagonally
1 tablespoon peanut oil	½ cup golden raisins
1 garlic clove, pressed	½ cup cashews
1 teaspoon grated fresh gingerroot	Salt
1 pound lean lamb tenderloin, cut into	Freshly ground black pepper
thin strips	2 teaspoons walnut oil

In a small measuring pitcher, combine the sherry, lemon zest, and sugar; set aside.

Heat the wok. Add the peanut oil and, when the oil is very hot and begins to smoke, add the garlic and ginger. Stir-fry 30 seconds. Add the lamb and stir-fry 3 to 4 minutes longer, or until brown. Add the sherry mixture and continue stir-frying 1 minute. Add the rice and stir 2 to 3 minutes, until it is warmed through.

Add the scallions and continue stir-frying 1 minute longer. Stir in the golden raisins and cashews. Season with salt and pepper to taste. Add the walnut oil and stir-fry 30 seconds. Serve at once.

Spicy Mango Beef

The combination of fresh mango and pickle makes this beef very special. It's best made when mangoes are in season, but you can still substitute canned ones. Look for mango pickle in Asian food stores. Serves 4.

4 tablespoons mango pickle	2 fresh mangoes, cut into large chunks with
1 pound boneless sirloin steak, cut into	skin removed
thin slices	Salt
1 tablespoon peanut oil	Freshly ground black pepper

Spread the mango pickle over the beef slices and let marinate 15 minutes.

Heat the wok. Add the peanut oil and, when the oil is very hot and begins to smoke, add the beef. Stir-fry 3 to 4 minutes.

Remove any excess pickle from the wok. Add the fresh mango pieces and gently stir-fry 1 to 2 minutes longer, being careful not to break up the mango pieces. Season with salt and pepper to taste.

Right: Duck and Orange

LAMB, SUGAR-SNAPS, AND MINT

The slightly sweet taste of the mint and the tang of the cilantro enhances the flavor of the lamb in this recipe. Serves 4.

2 tablespoons soy sauce	2 garlic cloves, pressed
2 tablespoons water	2 teaspoons grated fresh gingerroot
2 teaspoons cornstarch	⅓ cup pine nuts, roasted
1 tablespoon chopped fresh cilantro	7 ounces sugar-snap peas, trimmed
2 tablespoons peanut oil	3 sprigs fresh mint, chopped
1 pound lean lamb tenderloin, sliced	2 teaspoons sesame oil

In a small measuring pitcher, mix together the soy sauce, water, cornstarch, and half the cilantro; set aside.

Heat the wok. Add the peanut oil and, when the oil is very hot and begins to smoke, add the lamb. Stir-fry 2 to 3 minutes, or until it is brown. Add the garlic, ginger, and half the nuts and continue stir-frying 1 minute longer. Stir in the peas, the remaining cilantro, and all the mint. Stir-fry 2 minutes.

Remove the wok from the heat and stir in the soy sauce mixture. Return the wok to the heat and stir-fry 2 minutes longer. Add the sesame oil and stir 1 minute. Sprinkle with the remaining pine nuts and serve.

SWEET–AND–SOUR PORK

Truly a classic, this is best served with white rice. Serves 4.

1 tablespoon soy sauce	2 teaspoons grated fresh peeled gingerroot
1 tablespoon brown sugar	1 pound lean pork tenderloin, cut into strips
3 tablespoons malt or sherry vinegar	2 small carrots, thinly sliced diagonally
6 tablespoons pineapple juice	1 onion, finely chopped
1 tablespoon cornstarch	1 green bell pepper, seeded and cut into
2 tablespoons peanut oil	strips
1 garlic clove, pressed	2 tablespoons pineapple pieces

In a measuring pitcher, combine the soy sauce, brown sugar, vinegar, pineapple juice, and cornstarch; set aside.

Heat the wok. Add the peanut oil and, when the oil is very hot and begins to smoke, add the garlic and ginger. Stir-fry 30 seconds. Add the pork and continue stir-frying 3 to 4 minutes, until the pork is brown. Using a slotted spoon, remove the pork; set aside.

Reheat the wok. Add the carrots and onion and stir-fry 1 minute. Add the green pepper and continue stir-frying 2 to 3 minutes, until the vegetables are tender but still crisp.

Stir in the cornstarch mixture and stir-fry 2 minutes longer. Return the pork to the wok and continue stir-frying 2 minutes, or until hot. Add the pineapple pieces and stir-fry 2 minutes longer. Serve at once.

CALF LIVER AND MUSHROOMS

When cooking liver, never add salt until the end because it toughens the meat. This is delicious served with red Camargue rice from France, or with sliced boiled potatoes. Serves 4.

2 tablespoons all-purpose flour	1 onion, sliced into thin rings
Freshly ground black pepper	2 teaspoons sweet Hungarian paprika
1 pound calf liver, sliced into 1-inch	4 cups sliced chanterelle or button
strips	mushrooms
1 tablespoon peanut oil	½ to 1 cup beef stock

Season the flour with black pepper. Coat the strips of liver with the seasoned flour, shaking off any excess.

Heat the wok. Add the peanut oil and, when the oil is very hot and begins to smoke, add the onion and liver. Stir-fry 1 minute, or until the liver is brown. Add the paprika and stir-fry 1 minute longer. Add the mushrooms and stir-fry 1 minute. Add the stock and continue stir-frying until the sauce thickens.

DUCK AND NOODLES IN SOUP

This is a wonderful way to serve duck, and the crisp skin is worth fighting over! It is best made with fresh duck, but a frozen bird will taste good, too. Serves 4.

14 ounces duck breast, skinned and	1 red chili, seeded and thinly sliced
cut into ¼-inch strips (reserve the skin)	2 cups + 2 tablespoons water
1 tablespoon peanut oil	7 ounces choi sum, chopped
1 scallion, finely sliced	9 ounces Chinese egg noodles
9 thin slices peeled fresh gingerroot	

FOR THE MARINADE	
½ teaspoon salt	½ teaspoon cornstarch
½ teaspoon brown sugar	1½ tablespoons water
1 tablespoon light soy sauce	1 tablespoon peanut oil
1 teaspoon pale dry sherry	1 tablespoon sesame oil
5 turns of freshly ground black pepper	

In a large bowl, marinate the duck slices in the salt, sugar, soy sauce, sherry, pepper, cornstarch, and water 5 minutes. Add the peanut oil and sesame oil to the marinade and let stand 5 minutes longer.

Heat the wok. Add the peanut oil and, when the oil is very hot and begins to smoke, add the duck skin. Stir-fry 2 to 3 minutes, until golden and crisp. Using a slotted spoon, remove the skin from the wok; drain on paper towels. Wipe out the wok to remove the excess oil.

Reheat the wok. Add the duck and marinade, scallion, ginger, and chili and stir-fry 3 to 4 minutes, or until the duck is cooked through. Using a slotted spoon, remove the duck; set aside and keep warm. Add the water to the wok and bring to a boil. Add the choi sum and noodles and stir for 1 minute. Return the duck to the wok and stir 1 minute. Divide into 4 portions and serve with sliced duck skin on top.

Above: Garlic–Lamb with Rosemary

GARLIC–LAMB WITH ROSEMARY

Garlic and rosemary are a classic combination with lamb, but the addition of Pernod and rosemary oil makes this dish special. It is delicious served with herbed rice and a tossed green salad. Serves 4.

2 teaspoons Pernod or other aniseed liqueur	3 large sprigs fresh rosemary
2 teaspoons water	Salt
1 teaspoon cornstarch	Freshly ground black or red peppercorns
2 tablespoons peanut oil	1 teaspoon rosemary oil
1½ cups thinly sliced zucchini	1 tablespoon grated lemon zest
2 garlic cloves, finely chopped	
1 pound lean lamb tenderloin, cut across the grain into ½-inch thick slices	

In a small measuring pitcher, combine the Pernod, water, and cornstarch; set aside.

Heat the wok. Add 1 tablespoon of the peanut oil and, when the oil is very hot and begins to smoke, add the zucchini. Stir-fry 5 minutes, until brown. Transfer to a plate; set aside. Wipe the wok clean. Add the remaining oil and, when it is hot, add the garlic and stir 30 seconds. Add the lamb and rosemary and stir-fry 3 to 5 minutes, or until the lamb is brown. Stir in the cornstarch mixture and stir 1 minute. Remove the rosemary and add salt and pepper to taste. Stir-fry 1 minute longer. Add the rosemary oil and lemon zest and continue stir-frying 1 minute. Serve the lamb on rice, topped with the zucchini.

CURRIED NOODLES AND QUAIL EGGS

The quail eggs add an unusual and distinctive flavor to this dish. Use any type of noodle except vermicelli. Serves 4.

12 quail eggs	7 ounces asparagus, cut into 1¼-inch pieces
9 ounces Chinese egg noodles	4 teaspoons curry powder
1 pound pork tencderloin, cut into cubes	1 cup coconut milk
½ cup all-purpose flour	4 sprigs fresh cilantro
3 tablespoons peanut oil	

Boil the quail eggs 3 minutes. Remove them from the pan and immediately rinse them under cold water. Let cool, then peel off the shells.

Cook the noodles as directed on the package; drain and set aside.

Toss the pork pieces in the flour, shaking off any excess. Heat the wok. Add the peanut oil and, when the oil is very hot and begins to smoke, add the pork and asparagus. Stir-fry 2 to 3 minutes. Using a slotted spoon, remove the asparagus; set aside. Continue stir-frying the pork 2 to 3 minutes longer, or until golden brown. Remove from the wok and pat the pork dry with paper towels.

Wipe the remaining oil from the wok. Reheat the wok to a medium temperature. Add the curry powder and coconut milk and stir-fry 1 minute. Add the quail eggs, asparagus, and pork and continue cooking 1 to 2 minutes. Add the noodles and stir 1 minute longer. Serve garnished with cilantro.

HONEYED PORK

The combination of honey, ginger, and sesame seeds creates a delicious sweet-and-sour taste. This dish is best served with plain white rice and a tossed green salad. Serves 4.

2 tablespoons honey	1 garlic clove, pressed or finely chopped
2 tablespoons soy sauce	1 teaspoon grated fresh gingerroot
2 teaspoons Worcestershire sauce	1 pound pork tenderloin, sliced into strips
1 tablespoon pale dry sherry	2 scallions, thinly sliced diagonally
1 teaspoon cornstarch	2 tablespoons sesame seeds, roasted
1 tablespoon peanut oil	1 teaspoon sesame oil

In a small measuring pitcher, combine the honey, sauces, sherry, and cornstarch; set aside.

Heat the wok. Add the peanut oil and, when the oil is very hot and begins to smoke, add the garlic and ginger. Stir-fry 30 seconds. Add the pork and continue stir-frying 3 minutes. Stir in the cornstarch mixture and stir-fry 2 minutes longer. Add the scallions and stir-fry 1 minute. Add half the sesame seeds and stir 30 seconds, then add the sesame oil and stir 1 minute longer.

Remove the wok from the heat and sprinkle with the remaining sesame seeds before serving.

VEAL AND LIME CURRY

This is a medium curry which looks as delicious as it tastes. Serve it with white rice and finely sliced fresh red chili. Look for curry paste in Asian grocery stores. Serves 4.

1 tablespoon peanut oil
2 to 3 tablespoons red curry paste
1 pound boneless veal, cut into 1-inch square pieces
14 ounces baby corn-on-the-cob, halved
1¼ cups coconut milk

2 tablespoons grated lime zest
2 dried kaffir lime leaves
1 green chili, seeded and sliced into rings
1 tablespoon fish sauce
1 fresh red chili, seeded and sliced into thin rings

Heat the wok. Add the peanut oil and, when the oil is very hot and begins to smoke, stir in the curry paste. Stir-fry 30 seconds. Add the veal and continue stir-frying 3 to 4 minutes, or until cooked through. Add the corn, coconut milk, lime zest, lime leaves, green chili, and fish sauce and stir-fry 3 to 4 minutes longer, or until the liquid has reduced by a quarter. Sprinkle with the red chili rings.

MEXICAN STIR-FRIED BEEF

This mildly spicy recipe from south of the border is a good family dish. Serves 4.

1 tablespoon peanut oil
2 onions, finely chopped
2 garlic cloves, pressed
1 pound ground beef
¾ cup taco seasoning mix
2 (8-ounce) cans plum tomatoes

3 (8-ounce) cans red kidney beans
1 tablespoon cumin seeds, crushed
2 tablespoons bottled hot taco sauce
1 fresh red chili, seeded and very finely sliced

Heat the wok. Add the peanut oil and, when the oil is very hot and begins to smoke, add the onions and garlic. Stir-fry 2 minutes, or until the onions are soft. Add the beef and stir-fry 6 to 8 minutes. Stir in the taco seasoning mix, tomatoes, kidney beans, cumin, and hot taco sauce and continue stir-frying 5 minutes. Add the chili and stir-fry 1 minute longer.

PORK, BROCCOLI, AND OYSTER SAUCE

This recipe has a wonderfully subtle flavor and is quick and easy to prepare. It is best served with plain white rice. Serves 4.

1 pound pork tenderloin, cut into bite-size pieces
2 to 3 tablespoons bottled oyster sauce
2 tablespoons peanut oil

12 baby corn-on-the-cobs, cut diagonally into 1-inch pieces
7 ounces broccoli, cut into small florets
1 chili, seeded and finely sliced (optional)

Marinate the pork in the oyster sauce.

Heat the wok. Add the peanut oil and, when the oil is very hot, add the corn, broccoli, and chili, if using. Stir-fry 2 to 3 minutes. Add the pork and sauce and continue stir-frying 5 minutes, or until the pork is cooked through and the vegetables are tender but still crisp.

WARM CHICKEN SALAD

This is a delicious summer lunch dish that can also be served as a first course any time of the year. Serves 4.

3 boneless chicken breast halves, skinned
2 tablespoons mustard
Juice of ½ lemon
1 teaspoon cornstarch
2 slices bread
1 garlic clove, halved
2 tablespoons olive oil
1 tablespoon peanut oil

1 head Romaine lettuce, separated into leaves
25 cherry tomatoes
1 ripe avocado, stoned and diced
Salt
Freshly ground black pepper
Shaved Parmigiano-Reggiano
Fresh parsley leaves

Cut the chicken into ½-inch-wide strips. Marinate it 15 minutes in a nonreactive bowl with the mustard, lemon juice, and cornstarch. To make the croutons, toast the bread. Rub the toast with the garlic clove, then cut the toast into small cubes.

Heat the wok. Add the olive oil and, when the oil is very hot, add the toast cubes and stir-fry 1 minute, until golden. Remove from the wok and drain on paper towels.

Wipe out the wok and reheat. Add the peanut oil and, when oil is very hot and begins to smoke, add the chicken along with the marinade. Stir-fry 5 minutes. Add the lettuce, tomatoes, and avocado and stir-fry 1 minute longer. Season with salt and pepper.

Transfer the contents of the wok to a large serving dish. Garnish with the croutons, cheese, and parsley.

Above: Warm Chicken Salad

Veal, Eggplant, and Tomatoes

This colorful layered dish looks and tastes its best when served with a mixed green salad and white rice. Serves 4.

2 eggplants	1 tablespoon chopped orange and
Salt	mandarin zests
5 tablespoons peanut oil	1 tablespoon balsamic vinegar
3 garlic cloves, pressed	Freshly ground black pepper
2 onions, sliced into rings	1 pound boneless veal, cut into 2-inch cubes
2 (8 ounce) cans plum tomatoes	2 tablespoons chopped fresh basil

Cut the eggplants into ¼-inch-thick slices. Lay them on paper towels, sprinkle with salt, and leave for 10 minutes. Pat the eggplants dry with more paper towels. Meanwhile, heat the oven to 350°F.

Heat the wok. Add 2 to 3 tablespoons peanut oil and, when the oil is very hot and begins to smoke, add half of the garlic. Stir-fry 30 seconds; remove the garlic from the wok and discard it. Lay as many eggplant slices that will fit flat in the wok, moving them around until golden brown on one side. Turn them to brown the other side. Remove from the wok, drain on paper towels, and transfer to a serving dish and place in the oven to keep warm. Repeat until all the eggplant is cooked.

Wipe out the wok with paper towels and reheat, adding 1 tablespoon peanut oil. When the oil is very hot and begins to smoke, add the onions and stir-fry 2 to 3 minutes, or until they are translucent. Add the tomatoes, orange and mandarin zests and vinegar, season with pepper and stir until heated through. Remove all the ingredients from the wok and layer on top of the eggplants; return to the oven.

Wipe out the wok and reheat it. Add 1 tablespoon peanut oil and, when the oil is very hot and begins to smoke, add the veal and the rest of the garlic. Stir-fry 3 to 4 minutes, or until the veal is cooked through. Stir in the basil and season with salt and pepper. Remove from the wok and layer the veal on top of the eggplant and tomatoes. Serve at once.

Stir-Fried Quail with Quail Eggs and Oyster Mushrooms

This is an interesting blend of "East meets West." Serve with brown rice, to make the most of the garlic butter, and a green salad. Serves 4.

8 quail	3 garlic cloves, pressed
1 tablespoon honey	7 ounces oyster mushrooms
2 tablespoons hot water	6 tablespoons finely chopped fresh parsley
12 quail eggs	Salt
1 tablespoon peanut oil	Freshly ground black pepper
4 tablespoons butter	

With a heavy knife, cut out the backbone of each quail. Open up the quail and flatten it. Wipe inside and out. In a small measuring pitcher, mix the honey and water. Brush this over the quail.

Boil the quail eggs 3 minutes. Drain immediately and allow to cool before peeling off the shells; rinse well. Meanwhile, turn on the oven to its lowest setting.

Heat the wok. Add the peanut oil and, when the oil is very hot and begins to smoke, add as many of the quail as possible, laying them skin side up. Place the lid on the wok and cook 6 to 7 minutes. Turn the quail over and cook, covered, 2 to 3 more minutes to brown the skin. To check if the quail is cooked through, prick the thickest part of the thigh; if the juices run clear, the quail are done. Remove the quail from the wok and place in the warm oven while the remaining quail are being cooked.

Remove the wok from the heat and remove any excess oil; reserve oil. Reheat the wok. Add the butter and garlic and stir for 30 seconds. Add the mushrooms, the hard-boiled quail eggs, and parsley, and stir-fry 3 to 4 minutes. Layer this mixture over the quail. Pour the reserved oil over and season with salt and pepper to taste.

Turkey, Red-Currant Jelly, and Mint

This dish has a wonderful light, fresh flavor. It makes a terrific luncheon dish when served with a mixed green salad, or a main meal served with sliced boiled potatoes. Serves 4.

3 tablespoons red-currant jelly	1 tablespoon peanut oil
½ teaspoon cornstarch	10 sprigs mint, chopped
1 pound skinless turkey breast, sliced	
into strips	

In a large bowl, mix together the red-currant jelly and cornstarch. Add the turkey strips and let marinate 5 minutes.

Heat the wok. Add the peanut oil and, when the oil is very hot and begins to smoke, add the turkey along with the marinade. Stir-fry 3 to 5 minutes until the meat is well browned. Add the mint and continue

Right: Veal, Eggplant, and Tomatoes

LEMON–CHICKEN AND SWEET PEPPERS

The combination of lemon and mint gives a distinctive and fresh taste. Serve in roasted pepper shells with rice or sliced boiled potatoes and a fresh green salad. Serves 4.

1 pound skinless chicken breast, cut into bite-size pieces
Juice of 1 lemon
Grated zest of 1 lemon
Freshly ground black pepper
1 tablespoon peanut oil
½ cup seeded red bell pepper, cut into long strips
½ cup seeded green bell pepper, cut into long strips
½ cup seeded yellow or orange bell pepper, cut into long strips
3 tablespoons finely chopped fresh mint

In a large bowl, combine the chicken, lemon juice and zest, and black pepper.

Heat the wok. Add the peanut oil and, when the oil is very hot and begins to smoke, add the bell pepper strips. Stir-fry 1 minute. Stir in the chicken and continue stir-frying 4 to 5 minutes. Add the mint and stir-fry 1 minute longer, or until the chicken is cooked through.

STIR-FRIED PINEAPPLE AND BEEF

Probably the first time you've thought of these ingredients together, but you won't be disappointed when you try this dish. Best served with rice or noodles. Serves 4.

1 pound beef tenderloin, cut into 2½-inch strips
1 tablespoon peanut oil
1 garlic clove, finely chopped
1 teaspoon finely chopped peeled fresh gingerroot
2 scallions, finely sliced diagonally
1 red bell pepper, seeded and diced
1 fresh red chili, seeded and cut into thin rings
4 fresh or canned pineapple slices, cut into triangular chunks

FOR THE MARINADE
1 teaspoon cornstarch
2 tablespoons pale dry sherry
10 turns of freshly ground black pepper
1 teaspoon salt
2 tablespoons soy sauce
1 tablespoon water
2 tablespoons sesame oil

In a large nonreactive bowl, combine all the marinade ingredients. Add the beef and let marinate 15 to 20 minutes.

Heat the wok. Add the peanut oil and, when the oil is very hot and begins to smoke, add the garlic, ginger, and scallions. Stir-fry 1 minute. Add the beef along with the marinade, red pepper, and chili and stir-fry 3 to 4 minutes longer. Add the pineapple and continue stir-frying 2 minutes, or until the pineapple is hot and the beef is cooked to desired degree of doneness.

RED-CURRANT JELLY AND LAMB

The classic combination of mint and lamb in this dish has the added interest of the red-currant jelly. This is great served with wild rice. Serves 4.

4 tablespoons red-currant jelly
4 tablespoons finely chopped fresh mint
1 pound lamb tenderloin, cut across the grain into ½-inch-thick slices
1 tablespoon peanut oil
1½ cups string beans trimmed and cut into 1½-inch pieces

In a large bowl, combine the red-currant jelly and mint. Add the lamb and let marinate 15 minutes.

Heat the wok. Add the peanut oil and, when the oil is hot and begins to smoke, add the lamb along with the marinade. Stir-fry 2 to 3 minutes, or until the lamb is brown on both sides. Add the beans and and continue stir-frying 2 to 3 minutes longer, until the beans are cooked but still crisp.

TURKEY WITH WATER CHESTNUTS AND CHOI SUM

The crunchy texture of the water chestnuts complements the choi sum. Serve on its own or with noodles. Serves 4.

1 pound skinless turkey breast, sliced into strips
1 tablespoon peanut oil
1 teaspoon sesame oil
10 water chestnuts, drained, rinsed, and cut into ⅛-inch slices
5 ounces choi sum, stems removed and separated into leaves
Salt
Freshly ground black pepper

FOR THE MARINADE
½ teaspoon salt
1 tablespoon soy sauce
1 teaspoon pale dry sherry
3 turns of freshly ground black pepper
½ tespoon cornstarch
2 teaspoons water

In a large nonreactive bowl, mix together the marinade ingredients. Add the turkey and let marinate 15 minutes.

Heat the wok. Add the peanut and sesame oils. When the oils are very hot, add the turkey along with the marinade. Stir-fry 2 minutes. Add the water chestnuts and continue stir-frying 1 minute. Add the choi sum and stir-fry 2 minutes longer, until the leaves begin to wilt. Season with salt and pepper to taste.

Right: Lemon–Chicken and Sweet Peppers

SPICED PORK WITH APPLES

Pork and apples are a classic combination and they are greatly enhanced in this dish by the addition of cloves and cinnamon. This is delicious served with stir-fried red cabbage. Serves 4.

¾ cup plus 2 tablespoons white wine vinegar
¾ cup soft brown sugar
4 whole cloves
1 cinnamon stick, 1½ inches long
1¼ pounds dessert apples, peeled, cored, and cut into eighths

¾ cup raisins (optional)
1 pound pork tenderloin, cut into ¼-inch thick slices

In a small bowl, combine the vinegar and brown sugar.

Heat the wok to a low temperature. Add the vinegar and sugar and stir until the sugar dissolves. Add the cloves and cinnamon stick and bring to a simmer, stirring for 30 seconds; remove the cloves and cinnamon.

Add the apples and raisins, if using, and stir gently until the apples are tender but still firm. When they are ready, pour the syrup into a warm pitcher, leaving the apples in the wok. Add the pork slices and stir-fry about 4 minutes, or until the pork is cooked through. Pour the syrup over the pork and stir well.

CHICKEN AND ALMONDS

This combination is an ideal appetizer if more exotic flavors are being served later in the meal. It's best served with white rice. Serves 4.

1 tablespoon soy sauce
2 tablespoons pale dry sherry
2 teaspoons cornstarch
2 tablespoons peanut oil
1 pound chicken breast, sliced into strips
2 garlic cloves, pressed or finely chopped
1 teaspoon finely chopped fresh gingerroot

3 scallions, sliced diagonally
½ red bell pepper, seeded and cut into strips
½ green bell pepper, seeded and cut into strips
¼ cup sliced almonds, toasted
2 teaspoons sesame oil

In a small measuring pitcher, mix together the soy sauce, sherry, and cornstarch. Heat the wok. Add the peanut oil and, when the oil is very hot and begins to smoke, add the chicken. Stir-fry 3 minutes, or until the chicken turns white. Remove from the wok with a slotted spoon; set aside. Add the garlic and ginger to the wok and stir-fry 30 seconds. Stir in the scallions and the peppers and continue stir-frying 1 minute.

Remove the wok from the heat. Pour in the soy sauce mixture. Return to the heat and stir 1 minute. Add the chicken and the almonds and stir-fry 2 minutes longer. Stir in the sesame oil and continue stir-frying 1 minute.

CITRUS LAMB AND VEGETABLES

The combination of flavors in this recipe is delicious with just a hint of citrus to add extra piquancy. It's best served with white rice. Serves 4.

1 pound lamb tenderloin, cut into strips
1 teaspoon citrus or lemon pepper
1 tablespoon pale dry sherry
1 tablespoon fish sauce
1 tablespoon bottled oyster sauce
2 teaspoons cornstarch
1 tablespoon peanut oil
2 garlic cloves, finely chopped
2 teaspons grated peeled fresh gingerroot
1 cup carrot cut into 1-inch julienne strips

5 ounces snow peas, trimmed and cut into 1-inch pieces
½ red bell pepper, seeded and cut into 1-inch strips
½ green bell pepper, seeded and cut into 1-inch strips
3 scallions, finely sliced diagonally
1 teaspoons lemon myrtle oil

Dust the lamb in the citrus or lemon pepper; set aside. In a small measuring pitcher, combine the sherry, fish sauce, oyster sauce, and cornstarch. Meanwhile, turn on the oven to its lowest setting.

Heat the wok. Add the peanut oil and, when the oil is very hot and begins to smoke, add the garlic and ginger. Stir-fry 30 seconds. Add the lamb and stir-fry 3 to 4 minutes longer, until the meat is brown. Using a slotted spoon, remove the meat and place in the oven to keep warm.

Reheat the wok. Add the carrots, snow peas, and peppers and stir-fry 3 minutes. Stir in the cornstarch mixture and stir 2 minutes. Return the lamb to the wok and stir-fry 3 minutes longer. Add the scallions and stir 1 minute. Stir in the lemon myrtle oil and stir-fry 30 seconds.

LAMB, APRICOTS, AND CILANTRO

The sweetness of the apricots and the distinctive taste of the cilantro blend to create this wonderful dish. Serves 4.

1 tablespoon pale dry sherry
1 teaspoon cornstarch
1 tablespoon peanut oil
1 pound lamb tenderloin, sliced

1 onion, finely sliced
1 garlic clove, pressed or finely chopped
1 (9-ounce) can apricots in natural juice
1 tablespoon finely chopped fresh cilantro

In a small measuring pitcher, combine the sherry and cornstarch; set aside. Turn on the oven to its lowest setting.

Heat the wok. Add the peanut oil and, when the oil is very hot and begins to smoke, add the lamb. Stir-fry 3 minutes, or until the meat is brown and tender. Using a slotted spoon, transfer the lamb to a plate and place in the oven to keep warm.

Reheat the wok. Add the onion and garlic and stir-fry 2 minutes. Stir in the apricots and juice and continue stir-frying 3 minutes. Pour the cornstarch mixture over and stir 2 minutes. Add the lamb and stir-fry 1 minute. Stir in the cilantro and stir-fry 1 minute longer.

Above: *Chicken and Vegetables*

LAMB KIDNEYS, BACON, AND GARLIC

This is a spoil-yourself breakfast treat, or a terrific light lunch when served with a crisp green salad or on a simple bed of white rice. Serves 4.

1 pound lamb kidneys	*1 teaspoon brown sugar*
2 teaspoons Worcestershire sauce	*1 tablespoon peanut oil*
2 teaspoons cornstarch	*2 garlic cloves, pressed*
1 tablespoon pale dry sherry	*3 slices bacon, cut into strips*
1 tablespoon water	

To prepare the kidneys, remove the outer skins and with a mallet, pound the kidneys flat. Remove the knob of fat from the center and slice the kidneys thickly. Plunge them into boiling water for a few minutes. Drain and repeat this process again to remove any bitter taste. Pat the kidneys dry with paper towels; set aside.

In a small measuring pitcher, combine the Worcestershire sauce, cornstarch, sherry, water, and brown sugar.

Heat the wok. Add the peanut oil and, when the oil is very hot and begins to smoke, add the garlic. Stir-fry 30 seconds. Add the bacon and continue stir-frying 2 minutes. Add the kidneys and stir 1 minute. Add the cornstarch mixture and stir-fry 2 to 3 minutes longer, or until the kidneys are tender.

CHICKEN AND VEGETABLES

The easiest way to coat the chicken for this recipe is by placing it in a plastic bag along with the cornstarch. This terrific family-style dish will serve 6 if accompanied by brown rice or noodles.

1 cup + 2 tablespoons cornstarch	*¼ teaspoon Chinese five-spice powder*
1½ cups warm water	*2 carrots, finely sliced*
1 chicken bouillon cube	*1 cup broccoli florets*
2 boneless chicken breast halves, skinned	*3 ounces snow peas, sliced*
4 boneless chicken thighs, skinned	*5 ounces baby patty pan squash, quartered*
2 egg whites	*2 celery sticks, sliced diagonally*
5 tablespoons peanut oil	*1 red bell pepper, seeded and sliced*
1 garlic clove, finely chopped	*2 cups sliced mixed mushrooms*
½ tablespoons finely chopped fresh gingerroot	*2 tablespoons soy sauce*
1 onion, finely sliced	*2 teaspoons Worcestershire sauce*
6 scallions, cut into ½-inch pieces	

In a large measuring pitcher, mix together 2 tablespoons cornstarch, the water, and the chicken bouillon cube; set aside.

Slice the chicken into ½-inch-thick strips. Turn on the oven to its lowest setting.

Place the egg whites in a bowl and beat lightly with a fork until frothy. Toss the chicken in 1 cup cornstarch (see headnote), then dip the chicken into the egg whites; you will have to do this in several batches.

Heat the wok. Add 3 tablespoons peanut oil and, when the oil is very hot and begins to smoke, add the chicken, in batches, stirring until the chicken is tender. Drain well; set aside in the warm oven.

Add the remaining peanut oil to the wok and, when hot, add the garlic, ginger, onion, and scallions. Stir-fry 1 minute. Add the Chinese five-spice powder and stir-fry 30 seconds. Add the carrots, broccoli, snow peas, squash, celery, bell pepper, and mushrooms, in that order, and stir-fry 3 minutes longer, until the vegetables are tender but still crisp. Stir in the soy sauce and Worcestershire sauce.

Remove the wok from the heat and stir in the cornstarch mixture. Return the wok to the heat and stir-fry 2 minutes until thickened. Return the chicken to the wok and stir 1 minute longer. Serve immediately because the vegetables lose their crispness if they are left to stand.

Pork and Black Olives

This colorful dish tastes as good as it looks. Remember that soy sauce is salty, so taste before adding salt. Serves 4.

1 tablespoon pale dry sherry
1 tablespoon soy sauce
1 teaspoon cornstarch
1 tablespoon peanut oil
1 pound pork tenderloin, cut into bite-size pieces
4 ounces small snow peas, trimmed
1 red bell pepper, seeded and diced
10 to 12 black olives, pitted
1 teaspoon sesame oil
Salt
Freshly ground black pepper

In a small measuring pitcher combine the sherry, soy sauce, and cornstarch; set aside.

Heat the wok. Add the peanut oil and, when the oil is very hot and begins to smoke, add the pork. Stir-fry 2 to 3 minutes. Add the snow peas and bell pepper and stir 2 minutes.

Pour in the cornstarch mixture and stir 1 minute. Add the olives and stir 1 to 2 minutes, or until the vegetables are cooked but still crisp. Add the sesame oil and stir-fry 30 seconds. Season to taste with salt and pepper.

Garlic, Quail, and Vegetables

This looks and tastes fantastic and is impressive enough to serve at a dinner party. The contrasting textures of the chewy mushrooms and the crisp water chestnuts are delicious. Serves 4.

4 quail (1 per person)
Salt
Freshly ground black pepper
2 tablespoons bottled oyster sauce
1 tablespoon soy sauce
1 tablespoon pale dry sherry
1 tablespoon water
2 teaspoons cornstarch
1 tablespoon peanut oil
1 garlic clove, pressed
6 dried shiitake mushrooms, soaked for 20 minutes, squeezed and sliced, with hard stems removed
½ cup mixed red and green bell peppers, seeded and sliced into 1-inch pieces
2 ounces snow peas, trimmed and sliced into 1-inch pieces
1 (4-ounce) can water chestnuts, rinsed and sliced ⅛-inch thick

Rinse the quail and pat dry. Chop each into 4 to 6 pieces. (A Chinese cleaver is ideal for this procedure.) Place the quail in a large bowl and season with salt and freshly ground black pepper.

In a small measuring pitcher, combine the oyster sauce, soy sauce, sherry, water, and cornstarch; set aside. Turn on the oven to its lowest setting.

Heat the wok. Add the peanut oil and, when the oil is very hot and begins to smoke, add the garlic. Stir-fry 30 seconds. Add the quail pieces and stir-fry 4 to 5 minutes, until brown. Using a slotted spoon, transfer them to a plate and place in the oven to keep warm. (You may have to do this in two batches, depending on the size of your wok.)

Reheat the wok. Add the mushrooms, peppers, snow peas, and water chestnuts. Stir-fry 2 to 3 minutes. Stir in the cornstarch mixture and continue stirring 2 minutes. Add the quail pieces and stir-fry 2 to 3 minutes longer.

Red Chicken Curry

This is a medium curry and tastes best when served with plain white rice. Serves 4.

1 pound boneless chicken breast halves, cut into bite-size pieces
½ cup all-purpose flour
3 tablespoons peanut oil
1 to 2 tablespoons red curry paste
1¾ cups coconut milk
1½ tablespoons crunchy peanut butter
1 tablespoon bottled fish sauce
1 fresh red chili, seeded and finely chopped
Salt
Freshly ground black pepper
Fresh coconut shavings (optional)

Dust the chicken pieces with the flour, shaking off any excess. Turn on the oven to its lowest setting.

Heat the wok. Add the peanut oil and, when the oil is very hot and begins to smoke, add the chicken pieces. Stir-fry 3 to 4 minutes, or until brown. Using a slotted spoon, transfer the chicken to a plate and place in the oven to keep warm. Pour out any remaining oil and wipe the wok clean.

Reheat the wok and stir in the curry paste, stirring for 30 seconds. Stir in the coconut milk and peanut butter and continue stirring until the mixture starts to simmer. Add the fish sauce and the chili. Stir 2 to 3 minutes.

Return the chicken pieces to the wok and simmer until the chicken is hot. Season to taste with salt and pepper and sprinkle with the coconut shavings, if using.

Above: Red Chicken Curry

BEEF, OLIVES, AND MUSHROOMS

Pitted sliced olives are easier to eat, but whole olives make a spectacular presentation. The cooking time of the meat depends on how well done you prefer your steak. Allow two slices of beef per person. Serves 4.

2 tablespoons bottled oyster sauce	1 pound beef tenderloin, cut into
1 tablespoon dark soy sauce	½-inch-thick slices, seasoned with freshly
1 tablespoon pale dry sherry	ground black pepper
1 tablespoon water	1 cup broccoli florets
2 teaspoons cornstarch	1½ cups sliced button mushrooms
1 tablespoon peanut oil	12 to 18 black olives, sliced or left whole

In a small measuring pitcher, combine the oyster sauce, soy sauce, sherry, water, and cornstarch; set aside. Turn on the oven to its lowest setting.

Heat the wok. Add the peanut oil and, when the oil is very hot and begins to smoke, add the meat. Stir-fry 2 minutes, or until brown. Remove the beef from the wok with a slotted spoon; set aside in the oven.

Add the broccoli to the wok and stir 2 minutes. Add the mushrooms and continue stir-frying 2 minutes. Pour in the cornstarch mixture and continue stirring 1 minute. Add the olives and return the meat slices to the wok. Stir 1-2 minutes longer, until the meat is hot and cooked as desired.

MEXICAN-STYLE CHICKEN WINGS

This is a great family recipe—children love it because it's not too hot. Adjust the taco seasoning according to the degree of "heat" your family or guests enjoy. Serves 4.

6 to 8 tablespoons taco seasoning	2 (8 ounce) cans crushed tomatoes
8 tablespoons peanut oil	1 green chili, seeded, if desired, and cut
1½ pounds chicken wings	into thin rings
1 tablespoon olive oil	2 tablespoons bottled hot taco sauce
2 onions, roughly chopped	(optional)
2 (8 ounce) cans red kidney beans,	1 tablespoon cumin seeds, crushed
drained and rinsed	

Mix the taco seasoning with 6 tablespoons peanut oil. Coat the chicken with the mixture and let marinate 15 minutes; the longer it is left the hotter it becomes.

Heat the wok. Add the remaining peanut oil and, when the oil is very hot and begins to smoke, remove the chicken from the marinade with a slotted spoon and add the chicken to the wok. Stir-fry 6 to 8 minutes. Prick the thickest part of each chicken piece; the juices should run clear when it is cooked through. Remove the chicken from the wok and set aside on a warm plate. Wipe out the wok.

Reheat the wok to a medium heat and add the olive oil and onions. Stir-fry 2 minutes, or until the onions are translucent. Add the kidney beans, tomatoes, chili, taco sauce, if using, and cumin. Stir 3 to 4 minutes. Remove from the wok and place in a warm dish with the chicken wings on top.

LAMB WITH PLUM SAUCE

The piquant flavor of the sauce adds an extra taste to the lamb. This is best served with rice. Serves 4.

2 tablespoons bottled plum sauce	1 garlic clove, pressed
1 tablespoon pale dry sherry	1 pound lean lamb tenderloin, cut into
1 tablespoon water	½-inch-thick rounds
1 teaspoon cornstarch	4 ounces sugar-snap peas, trimmed
1 tablespoon peanut oil	1½ cups sliced button mushrooms

In a small measuring pitcher, combine the plum sauce, sherry, water, and cornstarch. Mix well. Turn on the oven to its lowest setting.

Heat the wok. Add the peanut oil and, when the oil is very hot and begins to smoke, add the garlic. Stir-fry 30 seconds. Add the lamb and stir-fry 3 minutes, or until brown. Using a slotted spoon, transfer the lamb to a plate; set aside in the oven.

Reheat the wok. Add the peas and mushrooms and stir-fry 2 to 3 minutes. Stir in the cornstarch mixture and continue stirring 1 minute. Add the lamb and stir-fry 2 to 3 minutes longer, until the vegetables are cooked but still crisp.

LEMON VEAL

The tang of lemon adds a wonderful flavor to the veal and the addition of myrtle oil makes it even more unusual. Serves 4.

2 teaspoons lemon juice	1 cup green beans, sliced diagonally
Grated zest of ½ lemon	into 1-inch pieces
2 teaspoons brown sugar	1½ cups thinly sliced button mushrooms
1 tablespoon pale dry sherry	3 scallions, sliced
1 teaspoon cornstarch	1 teaspoon lemon myrtle oil (optional)
1 tablespoon peanut oil	Citrus or lemon pepper
1 pound boneless veal, thinly sliced	

In a small measuring pitcher, combine the lemon juice and zest, brown sugar, sherry, and cornstarch.

Heat the wok. Add the peanut oil and, when the oil is very hot and begins to smoke, add the veal. Stir-fry 2 to 3 minutes, until brown and tender. Add the beans and continue stirring 1 minute, then add the mushrooms and stir-fry 2 minutes longer.

Pour in the cornstarch mixture and continue stirring 2 minutes. Add the scallions and stir 2 minutes, until the vegetables are cooked but still crisp. Stir through the lemon myrtle oil, if using, and add the citrus or lemon pepper to taste.

Right: Beef, Olives, and Mushrooms

CHICKEN, MUSHROOMS, AND BASIL

Use either sherry or vermouth in this dish—try both variations to decide which flavor you prefer. This is best served with Chinese egg noodles. Serves 4.

2 tablespoons peanut oil	4 ounces baby corn-on-the-cobs,
1 pound skinless chicken breast, sliced	sliced diagonally
2 leeks, finely sliced and rinsed	2 tablespoons pale dry sherry or white
2 cups mixed mushrooms	vermouth
½ red bell pepper, seeded and sliced	3 tablespoons lemon juice
½ yellow bell pepper, seeded and sliced	1 tablespoon chopped fresh parsley
8 cherry tomatoes	2 tablespoons chopped fresh basil

Turn on the oven to its lowest setting. Heat the wok. Add the peanut oil and, when the oil is very hot and begins to smoke, add the chicken. Stir-fry 3 minutes, or until the chicken turns white. Using a slotted spoon, transfer the chicken to a plate and place in the oven to keep warm.

Add the leeks, mushrooms, peppers, tomatoes, and corn to the wok and stir-fry 2 to 3 minutes, until the vegetables are tender but still crisp. Stir in the sherry, lemon juice, and herbs and continue stirring for 30 seconds. Return the chicken to the wok and stir 1 minute longer, until the chicken is very hot.

CITRUS PORK AND VEGETABLES

The slight tang of orange perfectly complements the pork. This is a great lunch dish that is best served with Brown Ginger Rice (see page 48). Serves 4.

2 tablespoons fresh orange juice	1 garlic clove, pressed
Grated zest of ½ orange	1 teaspoon grated fresh peeled gingerroot
1 tablespoon pale dry sherry	1 pound pork tenderloin, cut into strips
2 teaspoons soy sauce	1½ cups sliced button mushrooms
1 teaspoon cornstarch	1 cup thin green beans, cut diagonally into
1 teaspoon brown sugar	1¼-inch pieces
1 tablespoon peanut oil	

In a small measuring pitcher, combine the orange juice and zest, sherry, soy sauce, cornstarch, and brown sugar.

Heat the wok. Add the peanut oil and, when the oil is very hot and begins to smoke, add the garlic and ginger. Stir-fry 30 seconds. Add the pork and continue stirring 3 minutes, until brown. Add the mushrooms and beans and stir 2 minutes longer.

Pour in the cornstarch mixture and stir 3 minutes, or until the vegetables are cooked but still crisp.

GARLIC–CREAM CHICKEN WITH OYSTER MUSHROOMS

This dish is best served with noodles or sliced boiled potatoes.

1 pound boneless chicken breast, skinned	6 to 8 tablespoons light cream
and cut into bite-size pieces	4 tablespoons chopped fresh parsley
1 tablespoon peanut oil	Salt
3 cups sliced oyster mushrooms	Freshly ground black pepper
4 ounces soft garlic-herb cheese, such	
as Boursin	

Heat the wok. Add the peanut oil and when oil is very hot and begins to smoke, add the chicken. Stir-fry 4 minutes, or until the chicken turns white. Add the mushrooms and cheese and continue stirring 1 minute. Stir in 6 tablespoons cream and stir 2 minutes longer, adding a little more cream according to taste. Stir in the parsley and season to taste with salt and pepper.

DUCK AND OLIVES

The combination of duck and olives may be unusual but it is guaranteed to be delectable. Best accompanied by a green salad. Serves 4.

9 ounces Chinese egg noodles	1 tablespoon peanut oil
1 teaspoon pale dry sherry	25 mixed olives, pitted
½ teaspoon cornstarch	2 tablespoons brandy
2 sprigs fresh thyme	1 cup chicken stock
2 sprigs fresh rosemary	Salt
1 garlic clove, pressed	Freshly ground black pepper
14 ounces duck breast, cut into	
¼-inch-thick slices	

Cook the noodles as directed on the package. Drain; set aside and keep warm.

In a large bowl, combine the sherry, cornstarch, thyme, rosemary, and garlic; mix well. Add the duck and marinate 15 minutes.

Heat the wok. Add the peanut oil and, when the oil is very hot and begins to smoke, add the duck, along with the marinade and the olives. Stir-fry 1 minute.

Stir in the brandy and ignite. When the flame dies down, stir 2 to 3 minutes. Add the chicken stock and noodles and continue stirring 1 minute. Remove the rosemary and season to taste with salt and pepper.

Bring to a boil and let the liquid reduce slightly before serving.

Right: Chicken, Mushrooms, and Basil

Beef and Black Bean Sauce

This is a wonderfully aromatic dish due to the Chinese five-spice powder. Serves 4.

1 tablespoon soy sauce	1 teaspoon Chinese five-spice powder
1 tablespoon bottled black bean sauce	1 cup sliced asparagus spears
2 teaspoons cornstarch	1 cup sliced snow peas
1 tablespoon water	1 yellow bell pepper, seeded and sliced
2 tablespoons peanut oil	1 red bell pepper, seeded and sliced
1 pound boneless sirloin steak, cut into thin strips	Chopped fresh chili (optional)

In a small measuring pitcher, combine the soy sauce, black bean sauce, cornstarch, and water; set aside.

Heat the wok. Add the peanut oil and, when the oil is very hot and begins to smoke, add the meat. Stir-fry 3 to 4 minutes. Add the five-spice powder and vegetables and continue stirring 1 minute.

Remove the wok from the heat and stir in the cornstarch mixture. Return the wok to the heat and stir 1 minute, or until the vegetables are tender but still crisp.

Veal, Tomatoes, Leeks, and Basil

Tomatoes and basil are always a perfect combination. Serve this dish for lunch accompanied by a green salad, or for supper accompanied by brown rice. Serves 4.

1 tablespoon dry white vermouth	2 cups skinned, seeded, and chopped tomatoes
1 teaspoon cornstarch	
1 tablespoon peanut oil	2 tablespoons chopped fresh basil
1 garlic clove, finely chopped	1 tablespoon basil oil
1 pound boneless veal, thinly sliced	Salt
2 small leeks, sliced diagonally and rinsed	Freshly ground black pepper

In a small measuring pitcher, combine the vermouth and cornstarch; set aside.

Heat the wok. Add the peanut oil and, when the oil is hot and begins to smoke, add the garlic. Stir-fry 30 seconds. Add the veal and stir 2 to 3 minutes, until the veal is brown. Add the leeks and tomatoes and continue stirring 2 minutes.

Pour in the cornstarch mixture and stir 1 minute. Add the basil and stir 1 minute longer. Stir in the basil oil and season with salt and pepper to taste.

Chicken, Water Chestnuts, Asparagus, and Black Bean Sauce

This is a great combination of flavors and the crunchy texture of the water chestnuts adds interest. This is best served with white rice. Serves 4.

1 pound boneless chicken breast, skinned and cut into bite-size pieces	10 canned water chestnuts, rinsed well in cold water and cut in half
3 tablespoons bottled black bean sauce	12 asparagus spears, cut into 1½-inch pieces
1 tablespoon peanut oil	
1 fresh red chili, very finely sliced (optional)	

Marinate the chicken in the black bean sauce 15 minutes.

Heat the wok. Add the peanut oil and, when the oil is very hot and begins to smoke, add the chili, if using. Stir-fry 30 seconds. Add the chicken along with the marinade and continue stirring 1 minute. Add the water chestnuts and the asparagus and stir-fry 4 to 5 minutes, or until the chicken is cooked through and the vegetables are cooked but still crisp.

Citrus Beef

This is a delicious combination of sharp and sweet flavors. Serve this with rice or a green salad. Serves 4.

1 pound beef tenderloin, cut into ½-inch-thick slices	2 tablespoons soy sauce
	2 teaspoons cornstarch
1 teaspoon Chinese five-spice powder	2 tablespoons peanut oil
1 tablespoon orange juice	1 teaspoon grated fresh peeled gingerroot
Finely grated zest of 1 orange	4 ounces fresh asparagus tips
2 teaspoons brown sugar	2 teaspoons sesame oil
1 tablespoon pale dry sherry	

Season the beef with the Chinese five-spice powder. In a small measuring pitcher, combine the orange juice and zest, brown sugar, sherry, soy sauce, and cornstarch; set aside.

Heat the wok, add the peanut oil and, when the oil is very hot and begins to smoke, add the ginger and stir for 30 seconds. Add the meat and stir for 3-4 minutes, making sure both sides are browned. Remove the beef from the wok and set aside. Reheat the wok and add the cornstarch mixture. Stir for 1 minute. Add the asparagus and stir for 2-3 minutes. Return the meat to the wok and stir for 2 minutes. Add the sesame oil and stir for 1 minute.

Right: Beef and Black Bean Sauce

TURKEY WITH CITRUS–CRANBERRY SAUCE

The unusual combination of citrus and cranberries complements the turkey perfectly. Serves 4.

1 tablespoon grated or shredded citrus zest
6 tablespoons orange juice
2 tablespoons lemon juice
⅔ cup cranberry sauce
1 tablespoon pale dry sherry
2 teaspoons cornstarch

1 tablespoon peanut oil
1 pound boneless turkey breast, sliced
2 scallions, sliced diagonally
1½ cups zucchini sliced diagonally
Freshly ground red peppercorns

In a small measuring pitcher, combine the citrus zest and juices, cranberry sauce, sherry, and cornstarch; set aside.

Heat the wok. Add the peanut oil and, when the oil is very hot and begins to smoke, add the turkey. Stir-fry 3 to 4 minutes, or until the turkey is tender. Using a slotted spoon, remove the turkey from the wok; set aside.

Return the wok to the heat. Add the scallions and zucchini and stir-fry 2 minutes. Stir in the sauce mixture and continue stirring 1 minute. Return the turkey to the wok and stir-fry 2 minutes longer, or until hot. Season with freshly ground red pepper.

DUCK IN PLUM SAUCE

This dish is best served with boiled white rice and a fresh green salad. The duck crackling is a delicious addition. Serves 4.

1 pound boneless duck breast with its skin
1 tablespoon water
1 tablespoon pale dry sherry
3 tablespoons bottled plum sauce

2 tablespoons peanut oil
2 garlic cloves, crushed or sliced
3 to 4 scallions, sliced
1 tablespoon soy sauce (optional)

Remove the skin from the duck breast and thinly slice the skin and the meat. In a measuring pitcher, combine the the water, sherry, and plum sauce.

Heat a wok or large pan. Add 1 tablespoon of the oil. When it is hot and begins to smoke, add the duck skin and stir-fry 2 to 3 minutes, until golden brown and crisp. Remove from the wok with a slotted spoon and drain on paper towels; set aside.

Wipe the wok clean and reheat. Add the remaining oil and, when hot, add the garlic. Stir-fry 30 seconds, then add the duck meat and continue stir-frying 3 to 4 minutes, until the meat is brown. Pour in the plum sauce mixture and stir 2 minutes longer.

Add the scallions and stir-fry 1 minute. Stir in the soy sauce, if using. Remove from the heat and serve topped with the duck skin.

PORK WITH ASPARAGUS AND BLACK BEAN SAUCE

This is at its best in summer when the asparagus is fresh and in season. It makes a wonderful lunch dish when served with brown rice. Serves 4.

1 tablespoon peanut oil
1 pound lean boneless pork, cut into strips
4 tablespoons bottled black bean sauce
12 fresh asparagus stalks, cut into 1¼-inch pieces
½ red bell pepper, seeded and cut into long strips

½ yellow bell pepper, seeded and cut into long strips
Salt
Freshly ground black pepper

Heat the wok. Add the peanut oil and, when the oil is very hot and begins to smoke, add the pork and black bean sauce. Stir-fry 2 minutes. Add the asparagus and peppers and stir-fry 3 minutes longer, or until the vegetables are cooked but still crisp. Season to taste with salt and pepper and serve.

Right: Turkey with Citrus–Cranberry Sauce

FISH & SHELLFISH

Stir-frying is ideal for cooking fish and shellfish because the cooking time is so brief. As long as the pieces are small, they will cook in no time at all, and the seafood will retain its delicate flavor. Experiment with different types of fish and shellfish and always buy the freshest ingredients available.

FISH IN BLACK BEAN SAUCE

This is delicious served with Lemon Thai Rice (see page 46). Serves 4.

1 pound flounder fillet or cod, cut into bite-size pieces, any bones removed
3 to 4 tablespoons bottled black bean sauce
1 tablespoon peanut oil
½ red or orange bell pepper, seeded and cut into long strips
1 cup broccoli florets
Salt
Freshly ground black pepper

FOR THE SAUCE
2 tablespoons soy sauce
4 tablespoons fish stock
1 small red chili, seeded and cut into thin slices
5 thin slices peeled fresh gingerroot

Marinate the fish in the black bean sauce 10 minutes. In a small measuring pitcher, combine the sauce ingredients; set aside. Turn on the oven to its lowest setting.

Heat the wok. Add the peanut oil and, when the oil is very hot and begins to smoke, add the pepper and broccoli. Stir-fry 2 minutes. Add the sauce and continue stirring 2 to 3 minutes. Using a slotted spoon, remove the pepper and broccoli to a bowl and place in the oven to keep warm. Lower the heat under the wok and add the fish pieces, without the black bean marinade. Gently stir-fry 2 to 3 minutes, until the fish flakes apart easily. Season to taste and place the fish on serving plates with the hot vegetables.

Heat any remaining pan juices with the black bean marinade until very hot. Pour the sauce over the fish just before serving.

SHRIMP AND MANGO

What a delicious combination. This is a great first course or light lunch when served on its own, or add some rice and noodles to make a main meal. Serves 4.

12 jumbo shrimp or tiger prawns, peeled and deveined, tails left on
½ cup mango pickle
2 tablespoons peanut oil
2 fresh mangoes, peeled and cut into large pieces

In a large bowl, marinate the shrimp in the mango pickle 5 minutes; turn them over a few times for an even flavor.

Heat the wok. Add the peanut oil and, when the oil is very hot and begins to smoke, add the shrimp along with the marinade. Stir-fry 3 minutes. Using a slotted spoon, remove any pieces of mango pickle. Add the fresh mango and stir-fry 1 minute longer, or until the shrimp are pink and the mango is hot.

SALT AND PEPPER SQUID

Perfect as a finger food for a party, this can also be served as a first course for 4.

FOR THE BATTER
1 cup self-rising flour
½ teaspoon salt
⅔ cup water

2 tablespoons salt
10 turns of freshly ground black pepper
1 red chili, seeded and finely chopped
lemon wedges

1 pound squid bodies
4 to 6 tablespoons peanut oil, depending on the shape of the wok

Make the batter by mixing together the flour and salt, and then beat in the water; beat until smooth.

Clean the squid bodies, removing the head if necessary, and the hard cartilage. Cut the squid into ¼-inch-thick rings. Dip the squid rings into the batter.

Heat the wok. Add the peanut oil and, when the oil is very hot and begins to smoke, add the squid. Stir-fry 1 minute. Add the salt, pepper, and chili and stir-fry 2 minutes longer. Serve with lemon wedges.

Above: Tuna and Guacamole Salad

SHRIMP, SCALLOPS, SNOW PEAS, AND GINGER

For best results, keep all the pieces of seafood and vegetables the same size. This looks attractive and the ingredients cook evenly. (See picture page 9.)

9 ounces fresh scallops
1 tablespoon pale dry sherry
1 tablespoon soy sauce
1 teaspoon cornstarch
1 tablespoon peanut oil
1 tablespoon grated fresh peeled gingerroot

1 garlic clove, pressed
1 scallion, finely chopped
8 ounces snow peas, trimmed
1 red bell pepper, seeded and chopped
9 ounces large uncooked shrimp, shelled and deveined
2 teaspoons sesame oil

Wash and dry the scallops. In a small measuring pitcher, combine the sherry, soy sauce, and cornstarch; set aside.

Heat the wok or large pan. Add the peanut oil and, when the oil is very hot and begins to smoke, add the ginger, garlic, and scallion. Stir-fry 30 seconds. Add the snow peas and red pepper and stir-fry 1 minute. Add the shrimp and scallops and stir 1 minute longer.

Remove the pan from the heat and stir in the cornstarch mixture. Return the pan to the heat and stir 2 minutes, or until the scallops are firm and the shrimp turn pink. Stir in the sesame oil and stir 1 minute longer.

TUNA AND GUACAMOLE SALAD

Tuna with guacamole is simply fabulous and accompanied by the dressing with cilantro it has an extra tang. To make a good guacamole, it is important to taste-as-you-go and adjust accordingly. This is a quite delicious luncheon or light supper dish. Serves 4.

4 thick slices bread
2 tablespoons olive oil
1 garlic clove, peeled
4 tablespoons peanut oil
1 pound fresh tuna, cut into 1-inch cubes
5 ounces baby spinach (use whole leaves)
12 cherry tomatoes

FOR THE GUACAMOLE
1 large ripe avocado
1 to 2 garlic cloves, pressed
¼ teaspoon salt
Juice of 1 lemon

FOR THE DRESSING
4 tablespoons water
1½ tablespoons soy sauce
5 thin slices fresh peeled gingerroot
1 fresh red chili, seeded and finely sliced
Grated zest of 1 lemon
1 tablespoon finely chopped fresh cilantro
1 tablespoon pale dry sherry
Salt
Freshly ground black pepper

In a measuring pitcher, combine the dressing ingredients; let them stand 15 minutes to develop a full flavor. Toast the bread lightly. Brush it with olive oil and rub each piece with the garlic clove. Cut the toast into triangles.

Heat the wok. Add the peanut oil and, when the oil is very hot and begins to smoke, add the toast pieces. Stir-fry 1 to 2 minutes, until golden brown. Remove them and drain on paper towels. Wipe the wok clean.

For the guacamole, mash the avocado with the garlic and salt. Add the lemon juice and stir thoroughly.

Heat the wok. Add the remaining olive oil and, when the oil is hot, add the tuna and stir 1 to 2 minutes, or until pink in the middle, but not cooked through entirely. Using a slotted spoon, remove the tuna; set aside and keep warm.

Add the baby spinach leaves and tomatoes. Stir-fry 1 minute, until the spinach starts to darken and go slightly limp. Remove the wok from the heat.

Arrange the salad ingredients on a plate, add the tuna, croutons, and guacamole. Serve with a bowl of the dressing on the side.

SMOKED FISH WITH VEGETABLES

The combination of smoked fish and vegetables is delicious and is best served with plain white rice or Lemon Thai Rice (see page 46). Serves 4.

14 ounces smoked fish
1 tablespoon soy sauce
1 tablespoon pale dry sherry
2 tablespoons lemon juice
1 tablespoon peanut oil
5 ounces broccoli florets and stems

5 ounces thin green beans cut into 1½-inch pieces
4 ounces orange or red bell pepper, seeded and cut into 1-inch pieces
1 tablespoon scallion sliced diagonally
2 tablespoons finely snipped chives

Place the fish in a shallow pan of simmering water and poach 5 minutes, or until just cooked through. While the fish is cooking, in a small measuring pitcher, mix together the soy sauce, sherry, and lemon juice; set aside.

Remove the fish from the pan; drain well. Carefully cut into pieces about 1 by 1½ inches; set aside and cover to keep warm.

Heat the wok. Add the peanut oil and, when the oil is very hot and begins to smoke, add the broccoli, beans, and peppers. Stir-fry 1 minute. Add the scallions and stir 1 minute, or until the vegetables are tender but still crisp. Add the sauce mixture and stir 1 minute. Gently add the fish pieces and half of the chives and stir 1 minute, taking care not to break up the fish. Serve with the remaining chives sprinkled on top.

COD AND SHRIMP IN LIME SAUCE

Give an extra tang to fish with this lime sauce. This makes a ideal first course for 6 to 8, or a main course, served with rice or noodles, for 4.

4 uncooked jumbo shrimp or tiger prawns, shelled, deveined, and cut into large pieces
9 ounces cod fillet, cut into bite-size pieces
Juice and grated zest of 2 limes
1 tablespoon peanut oil
1 garlic clove, pressed

2 teaspoon grated fresh peeled gingerroot
1 tablespoon fish sauce
1 red chili, seeded and finely chopped
2 scallions, cut lengthwise into strips
2 tablespoons chopped fresh cilantro

Marinate the shrimp and cod in the lime juice and zest 30 minutes. Remove the shrimp and fish and pat dry with paper towels, reserving the liquid. Heat the oven to a low setting.

Heat the wok. Add the peanut oil and, when the oil is very hot and begins to smoke, add the garlic and ginger. Stir-fry 30 seconds. Add the shrimp and stir-fry 1 to 2 minutes longer, until they are translucent. Using a slotted spoon, remove the shrimp; set aside and cover to keep hot.

Add the cod to the wok and stir-fry 2 minutes. Remove and add the cod to the shrimp. Add the lime marinade, fish sauce, and chili to the wok, stirring until the liquid is slightly reduced. Pour the liquid over the hot shrimp and cod. Garnish with the scallions and fresh cilantro.

SHRIMP, CILANTRO, AND PESTO

These shrimp are fabulous—it's the taste of cilantro and pesto that makes all the difference. Serve on their own as a first course or with rice for lunch. Serves 4.

3 tablespoons olive oil
12 uncooked jumbo shrimp or tiger prawns, shelled and deveined, tails left on
4 tablespoons bottled pesto sauce

Small bunch fresh cilantro, finely chopped
Salt
Freshly ground black pepper

Heat the wok. Add the olive oil and, when the oil is hot and begins to smoke, add the shrimp, pesto, and cilantro. Stir-fry 30 seconds. Lower the heat and continue stir-frying 2 to 3 minutes until the shrimp turn pink. Season with salt and freshly ground pepper to taste.

Above: Shrimp, Cilantro, and Pesto

39

MUSSELS, COCONUT MILK, AND LEMONGRASS

The addition of lemongrass to mussels gives them an exceptional flavor. This is a delicious first course for 6, or it can be served as a main meal for 4 when accompanied by brown rice.

2¼ pounds fresh mussels
2 lemongrass stalks, cut into ½-inch pieces
¾ cup coconut milk

1 tablespoon fish sauce
½ cup small, fresh whole cilantro leaves

Clean the mussels well; discard any that are open and do not close when tapped with a knife. Crush the lemongrass to release the flavor.

Heat the wok. Add the coconut milk and lemongrass, bring to a boil, and let simmer and reduce 3 to 5 minutes. Increase the heat, add the mussels and the fish sauce, and cover the wok 1 minute. Uncover and stir until the mussels open; discard any that have not opened. Place the mussels in a large serving dish and add a small amount of the coconut milk. Sprinkle with the cilantro leaves.

GARLIC AND CHILI SHRIMP

A fabulous appetizer or light lunch dish. Fresh cilantro adds an exotic dimension to the shrimp. Delicious served on their own or with rice. Serves 4.

2 tablespoons peanut oil
3 garlic cloves, finely chopped
3 fresh red chilies, seeded and cut into very thin rings
12 uncooked jumbo shrimp or tiger prawns, shelled and deveined, tails left on

6 sprigs fresh cilantro leaves
Salt
Freshly ground black pepper

Heat the wok. Add the peanut oil and, when the oil is very hot and begins to smoke, add the garlic, chilies and shrimp. Stir-fry 5 minutes, or until the shrimp are pink and cooked through. Add the cilantro and season with salt and pepper to taste. Stir for 1 minute. Serve.

STIR-FRIED SNAPPER

Serve the snappers on a large plate for maximum effect. Serves 4.

2 large snappers, dressed and scaled
1 lemon
16 slices fresh peeled gingerroot
2 garlic cloves pressed

2 scallions (white part only—use the green part in the dressing), chopped
4 tablespoons finely chopped fresh cilantro
3 tablespoons olive oil
4 sprigs fresh cilantro

FOR THE DRESSING
4 tablespoons water
1½ tablespoons soy sauce
5 thin slices fresh peeled gingerroot
1 fresh red chili, seeded and finely sliced
Grated zest of 1 lemon
1 tablespoon finely chopped fresh cilantro

1 teaspoon pale dry sherry
5 turns of freshly ground black pepper
Pinch of salt
1 scallion (green part only), cut into matchsticks

Using a very sharp knife, score the skin of the snapper in 3 shallow strips or a diamond pattern. Stuff each fish with a lemon wedge, a few slices of the ginger, a clove of garlic, scallions, and finely chopped cilantro. Brush with the olive oil and marinate for 15 minutes.

In a measuring pitcher, mix the ingredients for the dressing; set aside.

Heat the wok. Add 1 to 2 tablespoons of the oil used in the marinade and, when it is hot, add the fish and gently stir-fry 5 to 7 minutes, until half cooked. Turn the fish over and continue stir-frying 5 to 7 minutes longer. When cooked, transfer to a warm plate.

Garnish the snappers with the cilantro sprigs and serve with the dressing.

HONEY AND CRACKED BLACK PEPPER SCALLOPS

The distinctive taste of the cilantro combines perfectly with the scallops. This is a great first course when served with Lemon Thai Rice (see page 46). Serves 4.

12 scallops, cleaned
4 tablespoons honey
1 tablespoon cracked black peppercorns
1 tablespoon hot water

1½ tablespoons peanut oil
2 teaspoons finely chopped fresh gingerroot
1 tablespoon finely chopped fresh cilantro

Marinate the scallops in the honey, black peppercorns, and water for 15 minutes.

Heat the wok. Add the peanut oil and, when the oil is very hot and begins to smoke, add the ginger. Stir-fry 30 seconds. Add the scallops along with the marinade. Stir-fry 3 minutes. Add the cilantro and stir-fry 2 minutes longer.

Right: Mussels, Coconut Milk, and Lemongrass

SQUID, GARLIC, AND BASIL

This method of cooking squid means it not only tastes good but also looks wonderfully different from squid rings. Serve the dish with noodles or bokchoy. This will serve 2 as a main meal or 4 as an appetizer.

1 pound squid, fresh or frozen
2 tablespoons bottled oyster sauce
2 tablespoons water
2 tablespoons peanut oil
2 garlic cloves, pressed or finely chopped

¼ cup roughly chopped fresh basil
½ teaspoon sea salt
1 small fresh red chili, seeded and finely chopped
Freshly ground black pepper

Split open the squid and remove the hard cartilage. Lay each squid flat and trim the wide end of any tough parts. Pat dry with paper towels. Make a small crisscross pattern all over the upper side—about ½-inch by ½-inch, taking care not to cut all the way through the flesh. Cut into 2-inch-square pieces.

In a small measuring pitcher, mix together the oyster sauce and water; set aside.

Heat the wok. Add the peanut oil and, when the oil is very hot and begins to smoke, add the squid. Stir-fry 1 minute; the pieces will fan out and begin to curl up into small tubes. Add the garlic, basil, and salt. Stir-fry 1 minute, or until the squid turns white. Add the sauce mixture and stir 1 minute longer. Stir in the chili and black pepper.

SCALLOPS AND VERMICELLI

The delicious aroma of Pernod and basil cannot be described. This is a perfect lunch or light supper dish served with a green salad. Serves 4.

12 scallops, cleaned
4 ounces vermicelli (or any thin pasta)
1 tablespoon olive oil
2 tablespoons finely chopped fresh basil

2¼ cups fish stock
4 tablespoons heavy cream
4 tablespoons Pernod or other aniseed-flavored liqueur

Cut the scallops in half horizontally. Cook the vermicelli as directed on package. Drain it well. Add the olive oil and basil; mix thoroughly and cover to keep hot.

Heat the wok. Add the fish stock and boil until reduced by half. Add the cream and Pernod and stir 30 seconds. Add the scallops and stir-fry 2 to 3 minutes. Pour over the hot vermicelli.

STIR-FRIED MONKFISH, CUCUMBER, AND MUSTARD

As Tim Withers, creator of this recipe, says, "It's a simple recipe but a great combination." Serves 4.

1 cucumber
Salt
16 to 20 ounces monkfish
About 1 cup all-purpose flour
Freshly ground black pepper
2 to 3 tablespoons peanut oil, depending on the amount of fish

FOR THE SAUCE
⅔ cup crème fraiche or sour cream
⅔ cup heavy cream
1 tablespoon whole grain mustard
A few dashes hot-pepper sauce

Seed and dice the cucumber, but do not peel. Sprinkle it with a little salt and let sit 30 minutes. Rinse it with cold water and drain.

Prepare the sauce by beating together the ingredients in a saucepan over a low heat until just heated through.

Cut the monkfish into even-sized strips. Season the flour with a little salt and pepper and dredge the monkfish in the flour.

Heat the wok. Add the peanut oil and, when the oil is very hot and begins to smoke, add the monkfish strips. Stir-fry 1 to 2 minutes. Add the cucumber and sauce to cover. Cook for a few seconds and serve on heated plates.

42

Right: Squid, Garlic, and Basil

RICE & NOODLES

Whether a main dish or accompaniment, rice and noodles are versatile stir-fry ingredients. They are ideal partners for rich or spicy sauces, and they give balance and bulk without detracting from the overall flavor of the dish. Plain white rice or simple egg noodles are best for serving with more complex flavors, or experiment with unusual types such as wild rice or Japanese buckwheat noodles.

FRESH TOMATOES AND NOODLES

The slight sweetness of this dish is delicious. Wonderful on its own, it also complements fish, meat, or poultry. Serves 4.

9 ounces Chinese egg noodles	1 teaspoon brown sugar
2 teaspoons walnut oil	Salt
11 ounces ripe tomatoes, peeled, seeded and chopped	Freshly ground black pepper
	1 tablespoon peanut oil
1 heaping tablespoon chopped fresh basil	3 garlic cloves, pressed
½ teaspoon fresh oregano	½ cup finely chopped leeks

Cook the noodles as directed on the package. Drain well and toss with the walnut oil.

In a bowl, combine the tomatoes, basil, oregano, brown sugar, and salt and pepper to taste.

Heat the wok. Add the peanut oil and, when the oil is very hot and begins to smoke, add the garlic. Stir-fry 30 seconds. Add the leeks and stir for 2 minutes. Add the noodles and continue stirring 2 minutes. Stir in the tomato mixture and stir 2 to 3 minutes longer, until the noodles are very hot. Season to taste.

EASY FRIED RICE

This no-nonsense dish is a delicious accompaniment to any meat, fish, or poultry dish. Serves 4.

1 tablespoon peanut oil	1 tablespoon finely chopped fresh cilantro
1 garlic clove, pressed	1 small red bell pepper or chili, seeded and very finely sliced
4 scallions, finely sliced diagonally	
1 cup white long-grain rice, cooked and cooled	1 teaspoon sesame oil
Salt	Freshly ground red peppercorns

Heat the wok. Add the peanut oil and, when the oil is very hot and begins to smoke, add the garlic. Stir-fry 30 seconds. Add the scallions and stir 1 minute. Stir in the rice and a little salt and stir 3 minutes, then add the cilantro and continue stirring 1 minute, or until the rice is very hot.

Stir in the red pepper or chili and stir 1 minute longer. Stir in the sesame oil and sprinkle with freshly ground red peppercorns.

WILD RICE WITH SUN-DRIED TOMATOES, PARSLEY, AND LEMON ZEST

Taste-as-you-cook with this dish, because measurements vary according to the amount of rice. This is delicious served on its own or as an accompaniment to poultry or fish. Serves 4.

1¼ to 1¾ cups wild rice	2 tablespoons grated lemon zest
4 to 6 tablespoons olive oil	Salt
10 sun-dried tomatoes in oil, drained	Freshly ground black pepper
5 tablespoons finely chopped fresh parsley	Shaved Parmigiano-Reggiano

Cook the rice following the directions on the package, because each brand is slightly different. Rinse well and leave to cool.

Heat the wok. Add the olive oil and, when the oil is very hot and begins to smoke, add the sun-dried tomatoes and the cooked rice. Stir-fry 1 to 2 minutes, adding the parsley and lemon zest. Season with salt and pepper to taste. Serve with the shavings of cheese on top.

BROWN LEMON RICE

Lemon myrtle oil makes this rice something really special so it's worth the effort to find some—look in health-food stores. Serves 4.

Juice of 1 lemon, freshly squeezed
Finely grated zest of 1 lemon
1 teaspoon sugar
1 tablespoon peanut oil
1 cup brown rice, cooked and cooled

1 tablespoon soy sauce
1 tablespoon chopped cilantro or parsley
1 teaspoon lemon myrtle oil
Freshly ground red peppercorns

In a small measuring pitcher, mix together the lemon juice and zest and sugar; set aside.

Heat the wok. Add the peanut oil and, when the oil is very hot and begins to smoke, add the rice. Stir-fry 3 minutes. Stir in the lemon mixture and continue stirring 2 minutes. Add the soy sauce and stir 1 minute. Add the cilantro and parsley and stir 2 minutes longer, or until the rice is very hot. Stir in the lemon myrtle oil and add the pepper to taste.

PINEAPPLE RICE

The addition of pineapple gives this super-quick recipe an unusual, fresh taste. Serve with chicken and pork. Serves 4.

4 slices fresh or canned pineapple
1½ cups water if using fresh pineapple, or juice from the canned pineapple

1¼ cups long-grain white rice
1 to 2 tablespoon peanut oil

If using fresh pineapple, remove the core and outer skin. Cut the meat into small chunks and soak in water 10 minutes. If using canned pineapple, drain well, reserving the juice, and cut into chunks.

Rinse the rice before cooking. Combine the pineapple juice and water and cook the rice as directed on the package. Drain well.

Heat the wok. Add the peanut oil and, when the oil is very hot and begins to smoke, add the rice and pineapple. If the rice sticks, add a little more oil, but the less oil used, the better the taste. Stir-fry 2 minutes, or until the rice is hot.

LEMON THAI RICE

With its lemon tang, this rice makes a perfect accompaniment to fish and seafood dishes. Serves 4.

Grated zest of 1 lemon
Juice of 1 lemon, freshly squeezed
1 to 2 teaspoons sugar
2 tablespoons peanut oil

1¼ cups long-grain white rice, cooked and cooled
½ cup golden raisins
½ cup slivered almonds, toasted

In a small measuring pitcher, combine the lemon zest and juice and the sugar; set aside.

Heat the wok. Add the peanut oil and, when the oil is very hot and begins to smoke, add the rice. Stir-fry 1 minute. Stir in the golden raisins, almonds, and lemon mixture and continue stirring 3 minutes, or until the rice is hot.

CHOW MEIN NOODLES

This is a classic recipe and a great family favorite. You may substitute any white meat for the chicken. This is best served with a green salad.

9 ounces Chinese egg noodles
1 pound boneless chicken meat, cut into strips
½ cup all-purpose flour
2 tablespoons peanut oil
2 tablespoons sesame oil
8 thin slices fresh peeled gingerroot
2 garlic cloves, pressed
2 scallions, white parts chopped
(use green parts, finely chopped for garnish)

14 ounces small shrimp, shelled
1 cup peas, fresh or frozen
2 tablespoons bottled oyster sauce

FOR THE SAUCE
⅔ cup chicken stock
1 tablespoon cornstarch
1 tablespoon soy sauce

Turn on the oven to its lowest setting. Cook the noodles as directed on the package. Drain well; set aside. Dredge the chicken in the flour and shake off any excess flour.

Combine the sauce ingredients in a measuring pitcher; set aside.

Heat the wok. Add the peanut oil and, when the oil is very hot, add the chicken. Stir-fry 3 to 4 minutes. Using a slotted spoon, remove the chicken, pat dry with paper towels and place in the oven to keep warm.

Wipe out the wok and reheat it. Add the sesame oil and, when the oil is hot, add the ginger, garlic and scallions. Stir-fry 1 minute. Add the chicken, shrimp, peas, and oyster sauce and continue stirring 2 minutes. Stir in the sauce mixture and stir 2 minutes, or until it is reduced by a quarter. Add the noodles and stir 1 to 2 minutes longer, or until they are hot. Serve topped with the green parts of the scallions.

Right: Brown Lemon Rice and Lemon Thai Rice

SWEET-AND-SOUR NOODLES

Always a popular combination of flavors, this recipe will be enjoyed by nonvegetarians as well as vegetarians. Serves 4.

4 ounces broccoli	3 tablespoons peanut oil
1 tablespoon cornstarch	1 red bell pepper, seeded and sliced
2 teaspoons brown sugar	1 green bell pepper, seeded and sliced
2 teaspoons bottled tomato sauce	1 large carrot, peeled and thinly sliced
1 pound canned pineapple pieces,	diagonally
with their juices	2 cups sliced button mushrooms
1 small fresh red chili, very finely sliced	2 scallions, finely sliced diagonally
9 ounces Chinese egg noodles	1 tablespoon sesame seeds
2 teaspoons sesame oil	

Cut broccoli into small florets and peel and slice the stems diagonally; set aside. In a measuring pitcher, combine the cornstarch, brown sugar, and tomato sauce. Stir in the pineapple and red chili.
Mix well.

Cook noodles following the directions on the package. Drain well and toss with the sesame oil, which will keep them from drying out until ready to use. Set aside.

Heat the wok. Add the peanut oil and, when the oil is very hot and begins to smoke, add the broccoli, peppers, carrot, and mushrooms. Stir-fry 3 minutes. Add noodles and continue stirring 2 minutes. Pour in sauce mixture and stir 4 minutes longer. Add scallions and sesame seeds and stir 1 minute.

BOLOGNESE NOODLES

This is a great alternative to Spaghetti Bolognese. It is quick and easy and makes a perfect winter lunch dish or a light supper for the whole family. Use whatever pasta or noodles you have in the cupboard. Serves 4.

9 ounces Chinese egg noodles	12 button mushrooms, sliced
1 tablespoon peanut oil	3 sprigs fresh thyme
2 garlic cloves, pressed	1 (16-ounce) can tomatoes
2 onions, roughly chopped	1 tablespoon tomato paste
1 pound ground beef	1 cup concentrated tomato soup
2 bay leaves	Parmigiano-Reggiano or cheddar cheese, grated

Turn on the oven to its lowest setting. Cook the noodles as directed on the package. Drain well, cover, and place in the oven to keep warm.

Heat the wok. Add the peanut oil and when the oil is very hot and begins to smoke, add the garlic and onions. Stir-fry 1-2 minutes, or until the onions are translucent. Stir in the beef, bay leaves, mushrooms, and thyme and continue stirring 5 to 6 minutes, or until the beef is cooked. Add the tomatoes, tomato paste, and tomato soup. Cook, stirring occasionally, for 4 to 5 minutes. Add the noodles, stir, and serve sprinkled with the grated cheese.

BROWN GINGER RICE

An excellent accompaniment to beef and lamb dishes. Remember to rinse the rice well before cooking so all the grains are separated. Serves 4.

1 tablespoon peanut oil	1 tablespoon soy sauce
1 garlic clove, pressed	1 tablespoon finely snipped fresh chives
1 teaspoon grated fresh peeled gingerroot	1 teaspoon walnut oil
1 cup brown rice, cooked and cooled	

Heat the wok. Add the peanut oil and, when the oil is very hot and begins to smoke, add the garlic. Stir-fry 30 seconds. Add the ginger and stir 30 seconds. Add the rice and stir 3 minutes longer, or until it is hot. Add the soy sauce and chives and stir for 1 minute. Stir in the walnut oil.

RED CAMARGUE RICE AND BACON

This rice, from the Camargue region of southern France, not only looks great with its distinctive color, but also has a delicious nutty flavor. Serves 4.

1 tablespoon peanut oil	½ green bell pepper, seeded and finely
1 garlic clove, pressed	chopped
1 teaspoon grated fresh peeled gingerroot	½ yellow or orange bell pepper, seeded and
1 cup red Camargue rice, cooked and cooled	finely chopped
3 slices lean bacon, diced	1 tablespoon soy sauce

Heat the wok. Add the peanut oil and, when the oil is very hot and begins to smoke, add the garlic and ginger. Stir-fry 30 seconds. Add the rice and continue stirring 3 minutes. Add the bacon and peppers and stir 2 minutes. Stir in the soy sauce and stir 3 minutes longer, or until the rice is very hot.

RED CAMARGUE RICE AND GARLIC

This is a delicious accompaniment to meat, poultry, and fish dishes, or even as a light meal on its own. Serves 4.

1 tablespoon peanut oil	1 teaspoon walnut oil
1 garlic clove, pressed	Sea salt
6 scallions, finely sliced diagonally	Freshly ground black pepper
1 cup red Camargue rice, cooked	
and cooled	

Heat the wok. Add the peanut oil and, when the oil is very hot and begins to smoke, add the garlic. Stir-fry 30 seconds. Add the scallions and stir 1 minute. Add the rice and continue stirring 3 to 4 minutes, or until the rice is very hot. Stir in the walnut oil for 30 seconds. Add salt and pepper to taste.

Right: Sweet-and-Sour Noodles

FRIED RICE COMBINATION

Fried rice is usually cooked with boiled and cooled rice (which can be kept covered in the refrigerator up to 4 days). This dries and separates the grains before frying to avoid a gluggy mess. This recipe serves 4—a good rule is to cook ¼ cup rice for each person.

1 tablespoon peanut oil
2 garlic cloves, pressed or finely chopped
1 cup long-grain white rice, cooked and cooled
¼ red bell pepper, seeded and diced
¼ yellow bell pepper, seeded and diced
1 cup sliced button mushrooms

2 ounces thick bacon slices or ham
½ cup peas, thawed if frozen
2 ounces small cooked shrimp
3 scallions, finely sliced diagonally
Salt
Freshly ground black pepper

Heat the wok. Add the peanut oil and, when the oil is very hot and begins to smoke, add the garlic. Stir-fry 30 seconds. Add the rice and stir 2 minutes. Add the peppers and stir 1 minute. Stir in the mushrooms, bacon, and peas and continue stirring 1 minute.

Add the shrimp and stir 1 minute. Add the scallions and salt and pepper to taste and stir 1 minute longer, or until the rice is very hot.

BROWN FRIED RICE

The nutty texture of brown rice makes a flavorful alternative to ordinary long-grain white rice. Remember, however, brown rice takes twice as long to cook as white. Serves 4.

2 tablespoons peanut oil
1½ cups sliced button mushrooms
6 scallions, finely sliced diagonally
½ red bell pepper, seeded and finely diced

½ green bell pepper, seeded and finely diced
1¼ cups brown rice, cooked and cooled
1 tablespoon soy sauce

Heat the wok. Add the peanut oil and, when the oil is very hot and begins to smoke, add the vegetables. Stir-fry 2 minutes. Add the rice and continue stirring 3 to 4 minutes, or until the vegetables are tender but still crisp. Add the soy sauce and stir 30 seconds longer, or until the rice is hot.

NOODLES AND FRESH HERBS

This tangy, sharp dish is a meal in itself, but it is also an excellent accompaniment to meat and poultry. Serves 4.

9 ounces Chinese egg noodles
1 teaspoon + 2 tablespoons basil oil
1 tablespoon peanut oil
3 garlic cloves, finely chopped
1 small red bell pepper, finely diced
1 heaping tablespoon chopped fresh basil

1 heaping tablespoon chopped fresh parsley
1 teaspoon chopped fresh tarragon
Grated zest of ½ lemon
Salt
Citrus pepper

Cook the noodles as directed on the package. Drain well and toss with 1 teaspoon basil oil.

Heat the wok. Add the peanut oil and, when the oil is very hot and begins to smoke, add the garlic and red pepper. Stir-fry 30 seconds. Add the noodles and continue stirring 2 to 3 minutes.

Stir in the herbs and lemon zest and stir 2 minutes, or until the noodles are very hot. Add the remaining basil oil and stir 1 minute longer, making sure all the noodles are coated with the oil. Season with salt and citrus pepper to taste.

NOODLES, SUN-DRIED TOMATOES, AND ASPARAGUS

This is a marvelous summer meal, when fresh asparagus is at its best. Fresh basil is just perfect with prosciutto and sun-dried tomatoes. Use any type of noodle except vermicelli. Serves 4.

4 slices bread, ideally olive or basil bread
Olive oil
9 ounces Chinese egg noodles
1 tablespoon basil oil
8 asparagus stalks, cut into 1½-inch pieces

12 sun-dried tomatoes preserved in oil, drained
4 slices prosciutto, cut into strips
6 tablespoons finely chopped fresh basil
Freshly grated Parmigiano-Reggiano
Freshly ground pepper

Heat the oven to 400°F. Brush the bread with olive oil, then slice into crouton-sized pieces. Place them on a baking sheet in the oven until golden brown. Let cool on paper towels.

Cook the noodles as directed on the package. Drain well; set aside.

Heat the wok. Add the basil oil and, when the oil is very hot and begins to smoke, add the asparagus. Stir-fry 3 to 4 minutes, or until almost cooked. Add the sun-dried tomatoes, prosciutto, basil, and noodles and continue stirring 1 minute. Serve with the croutons, cheese, and freshly ground pepper to taste.

Right: *Fried Rice Combination*

VEGETABLES

Most stir-fry recipes use large amounts of fresh seasonal vegetables. Try unusual Chinese varieties or a combination of old favorites with a new sauce or spices. Stir-fried vegetables taste delicious, are so easy to cook, and retain their color, texture, and nutritional value when they are stir-fried. Always slice vegetables for stir-frying diagonally because more of their surface comes into contact with the heat, cooking them faster.

STIR-FRIED VEGETABLE FONDUE

This is a great fun-dish for the family. It is very versatile and any vegetable can be used. Those listed below are especially good as they do not need to be cooked in advance and they retain their shapes. Use any combination on hand to make up the necessary weight.
Serves 4 to 6.

A combined weight of about 1 pound vegetables, such as cherry tomatoes, cauliflower, broccoli, green beans, asparagus, peppers, carrots, and celery
2 tablespoons olive oil

2 garlic cloves, peeled
3 sprigs fresh rosemary
2 teaspoons salt
10 turns of freshly ground black pepper
2 cups grated Swiss cheese

Rinse and chop the vegetables into bite-size pieces (leave cherry tomatoes whole). Turn on the oven to its lowest setting.

Heat the wok. Add the olive oil and, when the oil is very hot, add the garlic, rosemary, salt, pepper, and all the vegetables, except tomatoes, if using. Stir-fry 4 to 5 minutes. Add the tomatoes and stir 1 minute longer. Remove the rosemary.

Place the vegetables in a large hot dish; keep warm in the oven. Melt the cheese in a saucepan or a microwave. Do not remove the cheese from the saucepan until you are ready to eat as it cools very quickly.

Pour the cheese into a large bowl and serve as the dip for the vegetables.

ASPARAGUS, FAVA BEANS, AND MUSHROOMS

The tang of the lemon adds a fresh taste to the vegetables without overwhelming their natural flavors. Serves 4.

2 teaspoons freshly squeezed lemon juice
Grated zest of ½ lemon
1 teaspoon brown sugar
½ teaspoon citrus or lemon pepper
1 tablespoon peanut oil
1 garlic clove, pressed or finely chopped

2 slices lean bacon, chopped
2 cups fresh asparagus sliced diagonally into 1½-inch pieces
½ cup small shelled fava beans, outer skins removed from each bean
½ cup sliced button mushrooms

In a small measuring pitcher, combine the lemon juice and zest, brown sugar, and pepper.

Heat the wok. Add the peanut oil and, when the oil is very hot and begins to smoke, add the garlic. Stir-fry 30 seconds. Add the bacon and stir 1 minute. Stir in the asparagus and fava beans and continue stir-frying 2 minutes. Add the mushrooms and stir 2 minutes.

Stir in the lemon juice mixture and stir all the ingredients 2 minutes longer, or until the vegetables are cooked but still crisp.

SNOW PEAS, CARROTS, AND LIME

These vegetables have a delicious sweet flavor and are good to eat on their own or as an accompaniment to any meat or poultry dish.
Serves 4.

1 tablespoon lime juice
Grated zest of 1 lime
1 teaspoon brown sugar
1 tablespoon peanut oil

2 garlic cloves, pressed
1 cup carrots finely sliced diagonally
1 cup small whole snow peas, trimmed

In a small measuring pitcher, combine the lime juice and zest and brown sugar.

Heat the wok. Add the peanut oil and, when the oil is very hot and begins to smoke, add the garlic. Stir-fry 30 seconds. Stir in the lime mixture and continue stirring 1 minute. Add the carrots and stir 2 minutes. Add the snow peas and stir 2 to 3 minutes longer, or until the vegetables are cooked but still crisp.

CABBAGE, MUSHROOMS, AND BACON

This makes a delicious lunch dish or a side vegetable with traditional cuts of meat. Serves 4.

2 tablespoons peanut oil	5 cups finely shredded red, white, and
1 large red onion, finely chopped	Savoy cabbages
⅓ cup finely chopped bacon	3 cups sliced oyster and button mushrooms
2 garlic cloves, pressed or finely chopped	Freshly ground red peppercorns

Heat the wok. Add the peanut oil and, when the oil is very hot and begins to smoke, add the onion and bacon. Stir-fry 4 minutes. Add the garlic and continue stirring 2 minutes.

Add the cabbage and stir well, keeping the cabbage moving around in the pan 7 minutes. Add the mushrooms and stir 3 minutes longer. Season with the pepper to taste.

STIR-FRIED TOFU AND VEGETABLES

The creamy texture of the tofu contrasts well with the crisp and crunchy vegetables. Serves 4.

2 tablespoons peanut oil	1 green bell pepper, seeded and cut into
1 garlic clove, pressed	1-inch-square pieces
2 teaspoons grated fresh peeled gingerroot	1½ cups zucchini sliced diagonally
Dash of paprika	3 scallions, thinly sliced
2 tablespoons dark soy sauce	4 ounces canned bamboo shoots, drained
8 ounces tofu, cut into 1-inch squares	1½ cups sliced shiitake mushrooms
2 sprigs fresh rosemary	Pinch of Chinese five-spice powder
1 red bell pepper, seeded and cut into	Freshly ground black pepper
1-inch-square pieces	1 tablespoon pale dry sherry

Heat the wok. Add 1 tablespoon peanut oil and, when the oil is very hot and begins to smoke, add the garlic and 1 teaspoon ginger. Stir-fry 30 seconds. Add the paprika and 1 tablespoon soy sauce and stir-fry for 30 seconds longer.

Stir in the tofu and and continue stirring 3 minutes. Using a slotted spoon, remove the tofu, garlic, and ginger; set aside. Wipe out the wok and reheat it. Add 1 tablespoon peanut oil and, when the oil is very hot and begins to smoke, add the remaining ginger. Stir-fry 30 seconds. Add the rosemary and vegetables, Chinese five-spice powder and black pepper to taste. Stir 3 minutes.

Stir in the sherry and the remaining soy sauce and continue stirring 2 minutes. Return the tofu to the wok and stir 2 to 3 minutes, until hot. Remove the rosemary and serve.

OKRA AND TOMATOES

Wipe rather than rinse okra, or it will become too slippery to cook with. Serves 4.

1 tablespoon peanut oil	1 pound yellow or red tomatoes, skinned,
1 garlic clove, pressed or finely chopped	seeded, and chopped
1 onion, thinly sliced	Salt
4 cups okra trimmed and cut into 1-inch	Freshly ground black pepper
pieces	1 tablespoon chopped fresh cilantro
	(optional)

Heat the wok. Add the peanut oil and, when the oil is very hot and begins to smoke, add the garlic. Stir-fry 30 seconds. Add the onion and stir 2 minutes, or until it is soft but not brown. Stir in the okra, tomatoes, and salt and pepper to taste and continue stirring 3 to 4 minutes, until the okra is cooked but still crisp. Stir in the cilantro, if using, and serve.

MUSHROOMS, BEANS, AND RED PEPPERS

This is a wonderfully colorful vegetable dish that makes an unusual side dish to serve with traditionally prepared meat and poultry. Serves 4.

1 tablespoon peanut oil	½ red bell pepper, seeded and cut into
1 garlic clove, pressed or finely chopped	1-inch squares
3 cups thin green beans, sliced diagonally	1½ cups small button mushrooms, halved
into 1½-inch pieces	2 teaspoon sesame oil

Heat the wok. Add the peanut oil and, when the oil is very hot and begins to smoke, add the garlic. Stir-fry 30 seconds. Add the beans and red pepper and continue stirring 2 minutes. Add the mushrooms and stir 2 minutes longer, or until the vegetables are tender but still crisp. Add the sesame oil and stir 30 seconds.

Right: Cabbage, Mushrooms, and Bacon

Above: Bok choy, Garlic, and Oyster Sauce

BOK CHOY, GARLIC, AND OYSTER SAUCE

You should be able to buy bok choy from large supermarkets or Chinese grocery stores, but, if you can't find any, substitute Swiss chard, spinach, or Chinese cabbage. Bok choy is also sold labeled as white mustard cabbage. Serves 4.

1 tablespoon water	9 ounces bok choy, washed and well
2 tablespoons bottled oyster sauce	drained, tough stems removed and
1 teaspoon brown sugar	cut into 4 or 5 strips
1 tablespoon peanut oil	Diced fresh chili (optional)
2 garlic cloves, finely chopped	

In a small measuring pitcher, mix together the water, oyster sauce, and brown sugar; set aside.

Heat the wok. Add the peanut oil and, when the oil is very hot and begins to smoke, add the garlic. Stir-fry 30 seconds. Add the bok choy and stir 2 minutes. Stir in the sauce mixture and chili, if using, and stir 1 minute. Be very careful not to overcook this dish as the bok choy should still be crisp when served.

EGGPLANT, TOMATOES, AND CHINESE MUSHROOMS

Salting eggplant may be out of fashion but this process does keep them from absorbing moisture during cooking, resulting in a less soggy dish. Serves 4.

4 dried Chinese mushrooms	1 tablespoon soy sauce
4 cups diced eggplant	2 scallions, sliced
9 ounces tomatoes	Salt
About 2 tablespoons peanut oil	Freshly ground black pepper
2 garlic cloves, pressed	

Soak the dried mushrooms in tepid water 15 to 20 minutes to soften; drain, pat dry, and thinly slice. Sprinkle the eggplant with salt; let stand 20 minutes. Rinse well with cold water and pat dry with paper towels.

Meanwhile, blanch the tomatoes in boiling water for 1 minute to loosen the skin. Peel, seed, and chop coarsely.

Heat the wok. Add the peanut oil and, when the oil is very hot and begins to smoke, add the garlic. Stir-fry 30 seconds. Add the eggplant and stir-fry 6 to 7 minutes or until soft, adding more oil if necessary. Add the mushrooms and tomatoes and continue stirring 2 minutes. Add the soy sauce and stir 1 minute. Add the scallions and stir 1 minute longer. Season to taste with salt and pepper.

CARROTS, ZUCCHINI, AND WATERCRESS

This is a quick-and-easy combination that makes a great accompaniment to poultry or meat dishes. Serves 4.

1 tablespoon peanut oil	4 scallions, sliced diagonally
1½ cups carrots, cut into sticks 2 inches	1 tablespoon soy sauce
long and about ½-inch thick	1 bunch watercress
1½ cups zucchini cut as the carrots	2 teaspoons sesame seeds, toasted

Heat the the peanut oil and, when the oil is very hot and begins to smoke, add the carrots. Stir-fry 1 minute. Add the zucchini and scallions and continue stir-frying 2 to 3 minutes longer, or until the vegetables are tender but still crisp. Add the soy sauce and watercress and stir 1 minute longer. Stir in the sesame seeds, reserving a few to sprinkle on top.

Warm Mushroom Salad

Good on its own or as a scrumptious side salad with beef or lamb.
Serves 4.

9 ounces mixed salad leaves and baby
spinach
½ cup roughly chopped fresh mint
2 tablespoons butter
2 garlic cloves, pressed
4 cups halved mixed mushrooms

FOR THE DRESSING
2 tablespoons balsamic vinegar
⅔ cup olive oil
1 teaspoon mango chutney
Salt
Freshly ground black pepper

In a large bowl, combine the greens, and mint. Make the dressing by stirring all the ingredients together; do not add to the salad until the mushrooms are cooked.

Heat the wok to medium-high heat. Add the butter and garlic and stir-fry 1 minute. Add the mushrooms and stir-fry 4 minutes longer, or until tender.

Toss the greens with the dressing. Using a slotted spoon, remove the mushrooms from the wok and place them on the bed of salad. Season with salt and pepper to taste.

Vegetarian Stir-Fry with Fresh Herbs

Serves 4.

2 tablespoons peanut oil
1 cup mixed red, green, and orange bell
peppers, seeded and cut into 1¼-inch strips
1 cup julienned carrot
1 cup green beans, cut into 1¼-inch strips
1 cup fresh asparagus tips, cut diagonally
into 1¼-inch pieces
1 cup snow peas, sliced diagonally into
1¼-inch pieces

3 scallions, sliced diagonally
1 tablespoon finely chopped fresh basil
1 tablespoon finely chopped fresh parsley
½ teaspoon lemon juice
1 teaspoon basil oil
Salt
Freshly ground black pepper

Heat the wok. Add the peanut oil and, when the oil is very hot and begins to smoke, add the peppers, carrots, beans, asparagus, and snow peas, in that order. Stir fry 4 to 5 minutes. Add the scallions, basil, and parsley and continue stirring 1 minute, or until the vegetables are cooked but still crisp. Add the lemon juice and stir 30 seconds longer. Add the basil oil and stir 1 minute. Season to taste with salt and pepper.

Broccoli, Red Pepper, and Pine Nuts

Serves 4.

2 tablespoons fish sauce
2 tablespoons water
2 teaspoons brown sugar
2 tablespoons peanut oil
3 cups broccoli, cut into small florets
with stems sliced diagonally

1 red bell pepper, seeded and diced
6 scallions, sliced
½ cup roughly chopped fresh cilantro
leaves
2 teaspoons sesame oil
½ cup pine nuts, toasted

In a small measuring pitcher, combine the fish sauce, water, and brown sugar; set aside.

Heat the wok. Add the peanut oil and, when the oil is very hot and begins to smoke, add the broccoli. Stir-fry 1 minute. Add the red pepper, scallions, and cilantro and stir-fry 2 minutes. Stir in the fish sauce mixture and stir 2 to 3 minutes longer, or until the broccoli is tender but still crisp. Stir in the sesame oil and pine nuts. Serve immediately.

Above: Broccoli, Red Pepper, and Pine Nuts

BRUSSELS SPROUTS AND WALNUTS

A delicious and unusual preparation of an everyday vegetable. This is excellent with roasted or broiled meat. Serves 4.

2 tablespoons peanut oil
1 garlic clove, finely chopped or pressed
1 teaspoon grated fresh peeled gingerroot
1 pound small Brussels sprouts, whole or halved

2 tablespoons soy sauce
1 cup walnuts, roasted and halved or in large pieces
1 teaspoon walnut oil

Heat the wok. Add the peanut oil and, when the oil is very hot and begins to smoke, add the garlic and ginger. Stir-fry 30 seconds. Add the Brussels sprouts and continue stirring 3 minutes. Add the soy sauce and walnuts and stir-fry 4 to 5 minutes longer, or until the Brussels sprouts are cooked but still firm. Add the walnut oil and stir for 30 seconds.

MIXED MUSHROOMS WITH GARLIC AND HERBS

This is a stir-fried version of a perennial favorite. Use any type of fresh herbs you like as long as they are fresh—dried are not suitable for this recipe. Stir in a pat of butter just before serving for a richer flavor. Serves 4.

2 tablespoons peanut oil
1½ pounds mixed mushrooms, including shiitake, brown, oyster, and button, thinly sliced
1 to 2 garlic cloves, pressed

Several sprigs each fresh herbs, such as chervil, tarragon, parsley, and basil, leaves chopped
Salt
Freshly ground black pepper

Heat the wok. Add the peanut oil and, when the oil is very hot and begins to smoke, add the mushrooms. Stir-fry 2 to 3 minutes, until just cooked. Add the garlic and stir 1 minute longer. Add the herbs and stir until the mushrooms are just cooked through. Serve immediately.

CAULIFLOWER, PECANS, AND CILANTRO

A great twist on a standard vegetable dish. Serve it with broiled or roast meat. Serves 4.

2 tablespoons water
1 tablespoon pale dry sherry
1 tablespoon soy sauce
1 tablespoon peanut oil
2 garlic cloves, finely chopped or pressed

3 cups cauliflower florets
2 scallions, finely sliced diagonally
½ cup pecans, halved or left whole
1 teaspoon sesame oil

In a small measuring pitcher, combine the water, sherry, and soy sauce; set aside.

Heat the wok. Add the peanut oil and, when the oil is very hot and begins to smoke, add the garlic. Stir-fry 30 seconds. Add the cauliflower and stir-fry 2 to 3 minutes. Stir in the scallions and continue stir-frying 2 minutes.

Add the sauce mixture and stir 2 minutes. Add the nuts and stir 2 minutes longer, or until the cauliflower is cooked but still crisp. Stir in the sesame oil.

TOMATOES AND HERBS

If you can't find yellow tomatoes, use all red cherry tomatoes. Substitute whatever herbs are available: mint, when used instead of the chives, nicely complements the summery tomatoes. Serves 4.

1 tablespoon peanut oil
2 garlic cloves, pressed or finely chopped
9 ounces red cherry tomatoes
9 ounces yellow tomatoes

1 heaping tablespoon chopped fresh basil
1 heaping tablespoon snipped fresh chives
Salt
Freshly ground black pepper

Heat the wok. Add the peanut oil and, when the oil is very hot and begins to smoke, add the garlic. Stir-fry 1 minute. Add the cherry tomatoes and stir-fry 2 minutes. Stir in the yellow tomatoes and continue stirring 2 minutes, or until the tomatoes are hot; be careful not to allow the tomatoes to become too soft—keep them moving around the pan. Add salt and freshly ground black pepper to taste.

Right: Brussels Sprouts and Walnuts; and Cauliflower, Pecans, and Cilantro

VEGETABLE STIR-FRY

Serves 4.

2 tablespoons peanut oil
1 garlic clove, finely chopped
2 teaspoons grated fresh peeled gingerroot
1½ cups broccoli florets with stems sliced diagonally
1½ cups green beans, cut diagonally into 1½-inch pieces
1 red bell pepper, seeded and sliced into strips
1 yellow bell pepper, seeded and sliced into strips
2 cups halved buttom mushrooms

2 scallions, sliced
3 ounces bean sprouts
1 zucchini, quartered lengthwise and sliced
2 celery sticks, cut diagonally into 1¼-inch pieces
10 to 12 ripe olives, pitted
½ cup pine nuts, toasted
2 teaspoons soy sauce
1 tablespoon sesame oil
Freshly ground black pepper
Salt

Heat the wok. Add the peanut oil and, when the oil is very hot and begins to smoke, add the garlic and ginger. Stir-fry 1 minute. Add the broccoli and beans and stir 1 minute. Add the remaining vegetables and mushrooms, the olives, and half the pine nuts. Stir-fry 2 minutes longer, or until the vegetables are tender but still crisp.

Stir in the soy sauce and sesame oil and cook 1 minute. Season to taste with salt and pepper and sprinkle with the remaining pine nuts.

ZUCCHINI, TOMATOES, AND GARLIC

This exceptionally quick-and-easy dish will jazz up a simple meat or poultry dish. Serves 4.

1 tablespoon peanut oil
2 garlic cloves, finely chopped
3 cups zucchini sliced diagonally into 1-inch pieces

7 ounces small tomatoes, halved
Salt
Freshly ground black pepper

Heat the wok. Add the peanut oil and, when the oil is very hot and begins to smoke, add the garlic. Stir-fry 30 seconds. Add the zucchini and stir-fry 2 minutes. Stir in the tomatoes and continue stirring 2 to 3 minutes, or until the vegetables are tender but still crisp. Season with salt and freshly ground pepper to taste.

SPINACH WITH GARLIC

Spinach is regaining favor as a vegetable. This dish proves why. Serves 4.

1 tablespoon peanut oil
2 garlic cloves, finely chopped
2 slices lean bacon, thinly sliced

1 pound fresh spinach or chard leaves, washed and tough stems removed
2 tablespoons pine nuts, toasted

Heat the wok. Add the peanut oil and, when the oil is very hot and begins to smoke, add the garlic. Stir-fry 30 seconds. Add the bacon and stir 2 minutes, until the bacon is nearly crisp. Add the spinach and stir-fry 3 minutes longer, or until the spinach wilts. Add the pine nuts and stir 2 minutes.

Right: Vegetable Stir-Fry

INDEX

ACKNOWLEDGMENTS

I would like to thank Susan Haynes and Laura Washburn at Weidenfeld & Nicolson for all the support and help they have given me throughout this project. A special thank you to Clare Haynes for her enthusiastic support with testing, typing, and inspirational contributions to this book. Thanks also to Fruzzina and Justine Mainwaring, Nicholas Beechey, Janet Payne, and Tim Withers. To the staff at 3d Computer Systems, Chippenham, England, for saving my sanity and the future of my new computer. Last but not least, my sincere thanks to Michael Burton for his enduring support throughout this book and for encouraging me to "wok around the clock."

First published in the United States of America in 1997 by
RIZZOLI INTERNATIONAL PUBLICATIONS, INC.
300 Park Avenue South, New York, NY 10010

First published in Great Britain in 1997 by
George Weidenfeld & Nicolson Limited
The Orion Publishing Group

Text copyright © 1997 Weidenfeld & Nicolson
Photographs copyright © 1997 Robin Matthews

ISBN 0-8478-2019-X
LC 96-71423

Stylist: Roisin Nield
Home Economist: Emma Patmore
Designed by Paul Cooper

Printed and bound in Italy